Appendix Project
Talks and Essays

Kate Zambreno

semiotext(e)

Contents

This book is dedicated to my daughter, Leonora Gale.

Leo, I wrote much of this while you were napping on or near me, in the first year and a half of your life…

Appendix A

VARIATIONS OF MORNING

I. TODAY

This talk was advertised as being about "the book's impossibility and ongoingness," although when thinking through what I hoped to think through—what I call lately my writing practice—I can't move past the date of this event, March 16, 2017, which when I will be reading this, will be today.

It's a strange task, to write about today. It makes me think of the date paintings of On Kawara, his *Today* series. All week I have been flipping through the large, heavy catalogue of his retrospective. Over almost half a century, On Kawara made 3,000 paintings bearing only the date in which he made the painting. The painting was begun and finished on the same day. If he did not complete a painting by midnight he would destroy it. He had an elaborate system for coding and archiving these date paintings, involving storing them in a box with the newspaper of the day. In this way, a painting represents the process of an entire day. Occasionally, on a single day, he would make two or even three paintings. When he was out of town, he would make the

Talk given at Printed Matter, March 16, 2017

paintings in his hotel room, and the paintings then were of a smaller size. Those paintings were usually gray, as opposed to his typical black, or occasional red or blue. There were long stretches of time in which On Kawara produced a date painting every day.

I like thinking of how On Kawara worked all day on one painting. When I originally saw the retrospective at the Guggenheim, circling around the spiraling architecture of the space past various dates, I thought of his *Today* series as a footnote of sorts to a day, like one of his factual entries of who he met or what he read, something rendered quickly, that omits the entirety of a lived existence, or attempts to catalogue it in a disembodied way. I now realize that each date painting instead represents the deep and slow absorption and attention of a daily practice. How the artist had to let the paint dry layer after layer throughout a day. In the photo of his studio in the catalogue, we can see the hairdryer he dried them with, the filled ashtrays on various tables throughout the different rooms, and the methods of exactingness and measure, as he hand-painted the typography for each painting. So a date painting shows a date lived inside, working on the painting.

Perhaps a day where there are two date paintings were not important days to On Kawara at all, as I had previously assumed, but days spent meditating on the act of painting, on the immediacy and yet slowness of the present-tense. And once a day ends, like a painting, the day begins again. In this way time can be viewed as impersonal, layered, and somehow transcended. Or perhaps these dates with more than one date painting were charged days for the artist, in some form, so he must meditate even more, to transcend the day somehow, to structure it, through involved work and obsessive archiving. The date perhaps then becomes an object of contemplation for the artist, but also for us, as we stare at it.

In one of the catalogue essays for the On Kawara show, the writer Tom McCarthy invokes the beginning of Ingeborg Bachmann's *Malina*: "Today is a day only suicides can know." This is a passage that I've thought about often, and have tried to write about before. I like thinking about this meditation on *Today* in connection to On Kawara, and my attempt to write about On Kawara, and March 16, 2017. The impossibility of writing the day. Either *Today*, or that specific date, which returns, to another date, in another year.

When writing this talk, I think all day about this date, March 16.

It will be the fifteenth anniversary of my mother's death the day I am supposed to give this talk, or series of notes, March 16, today, yet I'm not supposed to be re-mourning, for the work that I've written about her is finished. And fifteen years is considered too long to mourn.

Actually—March 16 will be the day she really died, or stopped living, the day I am supposed to give this talk, but not the day preserved as the day she died. She died at night but her official date wasn't marked until the morning, March 17. (Still still—fifteen years later, I hold this grudge, against those who keep official records.)

I did not discourage the book on my mother that I worked on for thirteen years coming out the week of the anniversary of her death, or that this talk was scheduled on the fifteenth anniversary of her death. I certainly didn't request it. I did agree to it. I observed it, with some detachment, and wondered if that meant I had stopped mourning. The date has ceased its terrible pull, for some time, the past's performance. It is a fact to me now, this date, March 16. Although it's impossible not to meditate upon it. On the duration of my mourning, embodied by that book and the fact that I keep on writing to it.

I notice just now that my ticket for the On Kawara show is affixed to my bulletin board. That shows how much I sit at my desk lately, preferring lately instead the bed. The date I saw the show was March 23, 2015. That will be two years ago next week. How much has changed since that time. It's been almost two years since I thought maybe I'd write something about On Kawara, and have thought and journaled about his date paintings, and his meditation on the nature of time.

Today I am thinking about On Kawara, but I will not finish this text today. I will write at most a paragraph or two, and then work on it the next day. If I do not finish it, I will not destroy it, but I will want to, many times. Writing for me is a layered process like this. Like time and memory. (Or: perhaps writing has become for me, actually, time and memory.)

Once again, I envy the work of the painter, and how it can be wordless. To apply layer after layer. Meditating on one date. Or on the newspaper headlines. Or on nothing. How slow and long it takes me to think through all this. How long it's been that I've been working slowly. How language has become more difficult for me, over the years, and especially lately.

In his essay Tom McCarthy also asks, "Is On Kawara a writer?" And I like thinking about that question as well. The Guggenheim retrospective was titled by the artist as "Silence." Perhaps silence can actually be read as a form of writing, that recognizes language's failure, the impossibility and anemia of words. When wandering around the museum, I thought about not only On Kawara's frequency in one day, the times he painted twice or three times, but also the days and weeks where this ritual, and others, were abandoned. What makes an artist stop? What makes them begin again?

Besides the constant work on the paintings, On Kawara had many ongoing activities or rituals that utilized language as a form of silence, or the repetition of the same words as a form of silence—the mailing of travel postcards to friends indicating what time he woke up, the charting of movements as he traveled in New York City, the writing down of people he met, the archiving or journaling of the date paintings, and the sending of telegrams. From 1968–1979, over a decade, he recorded every day the series *I Got Up*, *I Went*, and *I Met*. This reminds me of Henry Darger's many modes of record-keeping, and how they accompanied his paintings, and structured his days, spent in so much solitude.

On Kawara's telegrams, sent to friends and business associates within the art world, stated simply I Am Still Alive. This project began in 1969, with three telegrams, three days apart.

They read:

I AM NOT GOING TO COMMIT SUICIDE DON'T WORRY
I AM NOT GOING TO COMMIT SUICIDE WORRY
I AM GOING TO SLEEP FORGET IT

A month later, he began to send out telegrams that stated only I AM STILL ALIVE. He sent out almost 900 telegrams, over three decades.

A meditation on time and the rituals of the day is also a meditation on mortality and death. On Kawara's retrospective was even more suffused with this awareness, since the artist died shortly before the show opened. So when we look at the collection of telegrams that state I Am Still Alive, this has ceased to be true.

II. A SORT OF BLACK WING (OF THE DEFINITIVE)

I've been rereading Roland Barthes's *Mourning Diary* again. To reread a book such as this becomes a form of memorial. To reread is a form of desire. A form of repetition, like mourning. And mourning, Barthes tells us here, is also a form of desire.

Beginning the night after his mother's death, Barthes began to keep a diary of aphoristic fragments, recording and philosophizing his mourning and its relationship to time. Not intending for the notes to be published (or at least not having edited them yet to be), the journal entries contain many repetitions, which mimic the returning and looping character of mourning, as it attempts and fails to be rendered into language. The fragmented form is partially dictated by what he wrote on, quartered pieces of typewriter paper that he kept on his desk.

A quartered piece of paper is about the size of one of On Kawara's telegraphs, although Kawara's telegraph series are the only documentations that the artist didn't handwrite himself, but dictated, given the conventions of the medium, and thus disturbing the controlled repetition that marks the rest of his work. In a reverse way, the handwritten and raw form of Barthes's *Mourning Diary* are in contrast to the critical yet ludic distance of his other work.

There is something of the immediate and photographic to these diary entries, that Hervé Guibert, in *Ghost Image*, his work on photography, mirroring Barthes's own work, calls "photographic writing," using as his example Kafka's last scrawls on paper, as he was dying of consumption in a sanatorium in Vienna, since he lost his voice, pieces that I think of as the silence scraps, but actually have been given a long German name in the Kafka lexicon, that I used to have written on a Post-It note on my desk, but now cannot find.

Barthes wrote a single entry on a scrap of paper the night after his mother's death, then nine entries the next day on October 27, seemingly all throughout that day. There are long periods in which he doesn't write these fragments, then he begins again, which signifies I think the way that mourning moves through time, how it circles and returns. The ritual of mourning, I think, involves both writing, and not writing, and is thus characterized by silence and a syncopation. Like On Kawara's date paintings, I'm interested in not only the frequency on a single date in the mourning diary but also the gaps between entries.

The journal, I think, is an activity or practice. Like mourning is an activity or practice.

In a catalogue essay the Guggenheim curator characterizes On Kawara's telegrams, with their noncontinuous nature, as an "urge," instead of the "routine" of the other documentary projects. Perhaps Barthes's mourning diary represents an urge, then, rather than a routine. Not the product of a meditative day, of order, but instead by the intensity of his emotions. On November 2 Barthes writes, after demarcating, "An evening with Marco": "I know now that my mourning will be *chaotic.*" (the emphasis is his).

Mourning Diary is a text narrating not only an event (the death of his mother) but a duration (the ongoingness of his solitude, without her). Barthes observes, over his two years of this practice, how grief works over time. How time can be distance, but also sudden closeness, how the awareness of her death becomes suddenly alive, much like a wound can be described as alive. He describes a scene at a library, an ordinary day, where suddenly, "a sort of black wing (of the definitive)" passes over him—a phrase that I find quite beautiful. That he realizes then again that she is dead, and that she will not return. The devastation of that.

It's the durational quality of my mourning that I still wish to give language to. That this book was a form of meditation that felt seasonal, cyclical. That if the book exists at all, it exists as a devotional object, that is undone, and that is ongoing. And how I repeatedly felt compelled to go back into it.

Mourning, Barthes theorizes through the diaries, is layered yet discontinuous. Time is also layered. Is mourning time? Time is linear (the days progress) but time is also chaotic (one cannot exist in the present-tense, in the day, one's work also leads to the past). Is mourning memory? Mourning is an interruption in time. A deferral from the present-tense. And yet it's also durational, about the day.

In his diary Roland Barthes whites out the day except for thoughts on his mother, which consume him. How one can have renewed mourning, a second and third mourning. Although he rejects repeatedly the psychoanalytic idea of mourning, of mourning as a process, hence linear, that can be gotten over, through. "Mourning: not diminished, not subject to erosion, to 'time.'"

I am giving another talk, next month, at a university, and to advertise the talk, the listing misspelled "mourning" as "morning," as in the beginning of the day. I liked thinking of that, of the relationship of mourning to time, which is the main meditation in *Mourning Diary*. I want to think about the grammar and tense of grief.

The "morning" of my mourning.
What time am I now in?
Can the mourning begin again?

Going through the anniversary every year. Did I find detachment over the date, with time? It's strange to remember a date. A date is really so impersonal. And it's too neat, to expect a memory to be triggered exactly on the same date. That's not really how memory works.

I can observe that this is the date, yet I do not wish to go deeper, to the specificity of my memories that I traced in the book.

The repetition of the phrase "Mon R! Mon R!" in *Mourning Diary*. This haunting refrain for him, perhaps his mother on her deathbed. At first when he writes this in *Mourning Diary*, he doesn't even spell out his name. And later, once a year passed, he can write his full name, the vocalization of her cry, he is still her child, his claim, "Mon Roland! Mon Roland!" It's unbearable to him, this cry. It's almost unbearable to me as the reader—the puncture of the intimacy of this scene.

As the anniversary approaches, Barthes fears in his diary that she will have to die another time for him. How religious that is. He spends the day at the empty white house at Urt, and feels empty. "The symbolism of the anniversary means nothing to me." How detached a date can be, how memory works in other strange, haunting ways.

How every Halloween, when I learned of her diagnosis, I relive it all again. Those five months of illness. In differing intensities, each year.

What compelled me to continually pick up this work again, after an absence? Something of the anniversary looming? What caused On Kawara to find a renewed interest in his date paintings, after an absence?

Every year is a new rotation around the sun. Last year, in this week, I found out I was pregnant, at 38 years old. Now, I'm 39, and I have a three month old baby, who is asleep on me, as I work through this, at 6am, her chin resting on my right breast, where she has just soothed herself, refusing to sleep, before finally relenting in that passionate, intense way of hers, her little mouth still moving in her sleep.

What I never anticipated is how much being pregnant, and having a baby, would change the nature of time for me, and how that would interfere with the mourning of my mother, which I thought was finished, since the book I wrote about her was finished. It has been one year since I found out I was pregnant, which was during this anniversary week of my mother's death, when I was thinking of her, and working again on the book about her, this time with a fervor I didn't quite understand, and which later I will attribute to hormones. It has been one year, but if you had told me it had been a decade, or five years, I would not be surprised. If you told me it has been five weeks, I would have been more surprised, but still accepting. My baby is almost four months old, but I feel she was just born, and that she's been alive forever. I am 39 years old, but I have never felt more the past year like I was a child, have never felt more strongly the absence of being a daughter, of having a mother. When I craved food, even before I knew, it was the comfort food of my childhood. The intensity of all of this has been closest to grief. Is it because of the exhaustion, or because I have never felt closer to life, and thus closer to death?

For there is a bliss in all of this to be sure. And Barthes writes again and again, that there is pleasure to his suffering. To exist in this strange state, of memory and the confusion of time, is to be alive.

"I live in my suffering and that makes me happy."

"Anything that keeps me from living in my suffering is unbearable to me."

The next day, a repetition:

"I ask for nothing but to live in my suffering."

We play this one Brian Eno composition when my baby sleeps, or to get her to sleep, that we found knocks her out. Sometimes we will have it on constantly, often because we forget to turn it off or don't realize it's playing, which I'm sure unnerves our upstairs neighbors. Sometimes I am so sick of this piece of music I cannot listen to it anymore, even though I used to love it, its loops and stillness. Or we play a white noise recording with its repetitive shushing sound that is supposed to mimic the noises she heard when in the womb.

You can imagine then this talk being written with the trancelike nature of the sound that protects our silence—the looplike repetition.

This altered state, I have been realizing, this raw and porous tenderness, is closest to grief. How unreal everything feels. How blissful at the same time. How the exhaustion enhances this bliss somehow, as well as this feeling of unreality.

There's a specific solitude and interiority in this period, this transformative present-tense, that condition that Barthes says is necessary in order to write, that he realizes at some point his grief might have allowed for. I sit in the bed in the near dark while the baby naps, usually on me or around my person, and attempt to read *Mourning Diary*, feeling somewhat like Albrecht Dürer's angel in "Melencolia I," an image open on my desk that I've been meditating on for two years, in a book I am supposed to write, that remains unwritten. The notebooks scattered around me on the bed, as I nurse the baby all day, my various Barthes books, *The Neutral, Camera Lucida, Mourning Diary*.

Imagine also this talk written in bed, over a period of several weeks, throughout the pockets of the day and early evening, little notes, scraps, and fragments, in a gray notebook that is repeatedly unable to be located. Then imagine these fragments instead written on quartered typewriter pages, or typed on telegrams.

When I write friends, I mostly report how much sleep I've been getting, the fragmented nature of my exhaustion. That the day repeats, is ongoing, becomes more pronounced somehow when you have a baby, when you begin religiously observing daily events like naps, and length of sleep.

For a baby to be considered sleeping through the night, it turns out, doesn't actually mean sleeping continuously, but sleeping for five or six hours, which is not actually sleeping through the night, but now waking up at 1am for a feeding. For the past week we have been waking at 1am, at 3am, and at 5am, for me to feed her, and sometimes when we're lucky we have been able to get her to sleep an hour or so longer and she's up at 6am or 6:30am. The Internet, that contradictory oracle, tells us to work on sleep rituals. To put the baby to bed at the same time, which used to be 10pm and as the months have progressed has moved earlier, now at 7pm, to bathe her and read her a little book, all so she knows the day versus the night, and begins to know that the night is when she's supposed to sleep. It was just daylight savings time, and she woke for the last time, unsettled in her crib, off the side of the bed, at 5am, which we thought at first was pretty good, but then realized that it was actually 4am, or at least felt like 4am. At this time in the morning we can sometimes struggle to get her to go back to sleep, by putting on the music we play to get her to fall asleep, and by shooshing her, and turning the lights down low, and putting her in the swing, but often she's up, and playful, and we have to turn the lights on and grind the coffee and go about our day.

Last night, however, it felt like she woke up every hour. She was up at 8pm, cooing and wanting to play and engage for two hours. Then she was up at 11pm. Then she was up at 12:30pm. Then finally, a patch of sleep for about four hours, and then up at 5am, and no more sleep after that. And each time she awoke, she screamed. She would not be soothed. I consult the Internet and the Internet tells me she's entering her four-month sleep regression, where she will begin to wake up more continually, where she goes back to needing more reassurance or sustenance in the night. It will last for at least a month, until there are later sleep regressions in the years to come. We cannot expect her to just continue in a deep sleep for the entire time she is sleeping anymore. She will fall asleep in our arms, and then she will wake up, scared and upset, perhaps worried she's been moved, which she usually has, on to a pillow on my lap or the swing, or sometimes the crib, and then we have to soothe her, either cradling her or holding her little hand, with her infinitely tiny wrist encircled in fat, or rubbing her belly, or soothing her on my breast, or more often, just waiting, and then she will suddenly pass out, after a theater of small yet specific cries like bleating yelps of protest, surrendering back to sleep, often after a fart or two. I had never really realized before how sleep is punctuated by ruptures, that it is something we continually wake up from, that there are layers to our sleep, of depth and lightness, where we have to assess our environment and make sure that we are okay.

That sleep is not linear, that it regresses, much like grief. It returns.

IV. THE WIRELIKE SHARPNESS OF MOURNING

Barthes gave a series of talks at the Collège de France over a series
of figures he thought of as embodying the disruptive and desired
affect of "the neutral," such as silence or sleep. The talks were
given over thirteen weeks, from February 18 to June 3, 1978. The
back copy of the English translation notes that this period was the
last two years of Barthes's life, so the two years before his death,
but it is also true to say that this was during his period of mourning
his mother, which also coincided with this transformative period
of work. In February of 1978, he is working on his mourning
diary as a sort of footnote to his work, which traces his desire to
write a novel, and his work on photography, which he referred to
as his work on his mother, which he did finish. In February of
1978, he is within only months of his mother's death. Perhaps we
can describe this as the early afternoon of his mourning. When
reading *The Neutral*, in the passive and yet passionate way I've
been going through all of Barthes, or reading anything, really, I
note the way mourning suffuses this text, in margined titles and
asides, much like mourning and also mortality suffuses all of his
texts of this period, the two years following his mother's death.
The lecture is quite fragmented, a series of notes, which embodies
a spirit I think of the neutral, if I understand it correctly. On this
first lecture, February 18, 1978, he speaks to the experience I feel
reading Barthes lately. "To read the dead author is, for me, to be
alive, for I am shattered, torn by the awareness of the contradiction
between the intense life of his text and the sadness of knowing he

is dead: I am always saddened by the death of an author, moved by the story of the death of authors (Tolstoy, Gide). To mourn is to be alive."

I feel this too when I'm reading through Barthes, especially his *Mourning Diary*. That reading him mourning his mother I am also mourning Barthes. Reading *Mourning Diary* is like a series of texts stating I Am Still Alive. Barthes is writing this, thinking through his mother, and I am reading this, thinking through Barthes. Knowing that his life would be cut short in a freak accident, hit by a laundry van on a Paris afternoon, crossing the sidewalk, after having lunch with future president of France, François Mitterand. On February 25, 1980, two years after giving his opening lecture on "the neutral." He had already stopped his mourning diary the previous September, though that is not to say that he stopped his mourning. Although the later entries become anemic, they are repetitive in their extreme sadness.

In fact his last entry is simply, "There are mornings so sad…" Perhaps morning is the time for mourning. For when you are asleep, you can imagine that the person you love, who lived your life with you, is still alive. Or you forget. It's funny how often, fifteen years later, I still forget.

In these later entries, Barthes writes repeatedly of his dreams of his mother. He doesn't describe these dreams, only that they are dreams, and they fill him with suffering (in the diary he distinguishes mourning from suffering, preferring the latter parlance. *Mourning* is too psychoanalytic, he writes). If he were to continue living, that is if he had not died, I would imagine he would have continued to dream of his mother. I imagine this because it is true for me. My dreams of her…they were once in my mother text, all the different ways I dreamed of her. How constant they still are for me. In some of them she is suffering, and in others, she is not suffering. In some she is fragmented and in others she is whole. Sometimes I am aware that she has returned, and in others she was always there. I know that I will dream of her until I die. And yet, when I dream of her, she will be at most the age she was when she died, which was 55. My imagination refuses to push past that. And with each year, I will be older and older. I seldom remember these dreams, like all of my dreams. That I could have them only once a year, or during stressful times. Perhaps I dream them every night. I feel certain I dreamed them more when I was pregnant, especially in the last weeks. Although my dreaming was often during the day, when I was awake. This portal that opened for me between dream and day. When the door opened, to my childhood. How I would have the urge all the time to talk to her, forgetting that she was no longer there.

The boredom that emanated these last years for Barthes (an entry he writes: "I'm bored wherever *I* am"). How he was bound up in dalliances that he refers to obliquely as diversions in the diaries. How the last two months of his life he spent proofing and editing *Camera Lucida*, his book on photography that is his book on his mother, and the despair he sunk into after "hostile" reviews. For having a book published is also another sort of death—this I understand, the dread and dissatisfaction of this as well. I wonder if that is why he stopped writing the mourning diary, because the other work, the book on his mother, was finished, so he felt he was supposed to move on, even though he found himself unable to do so. Maybe he became bored with the repetition of his entries, how boring and banal mourning actually is, which he gives language to. It is clear from the entries at the end how intensely in pain he still was, and yet he stopped being able to give it language or narrative, to live in memories. He refers to the muteness of his grief and suffering.

He issues a caveat, in this February 18 first *Neutral* lecture, first laying out that the neutral is something he desires. In a sub-section entitled, beautifully, "The Wirelike Sharpness of Mourning," a non-neutral affect, he notes that he came up with the subject of his course before a non-named "serious event" entered his life, and that he is transformed, as a subject.

I look at the February 18, 1978 entry in *Mourning Diary*, trying to relocate him, as he began these lectures. There are two entries from that day, and then one very brief entry two days later, noting that he is sick with bronchitis, and then no more entries for several weeks, one of his many ebbs and flows. The entry, a repetition of ideas before (like this talk, I keep on repeating).

Feb 18, 1978
"Mourning: I've learned that it was inimitable and sporadic it does not wear away, because it's not continuous."

Later, he writes:

"But if these 'changes' (which account for what is sporadic) make for silence, inwardness, the wound of mourning shifts towards a higher realm of thought."

These ideas repeat throughout his diaries, reflecting on not only the discontinuous, chaotic, and immobile character of mourning, but also how grieving can be a form of writing, if one is allowed interiority, and silence, these merits of the neutral.

In that same initial lecture on "the neutral," Barthes speaks to exhaustion, what he calls weariness, as a specific, disruptive, refusal. Mourning again appears as a parenthetical in the text. In his beginning ruminations on Weariness, he muses, hypothetically of course, what specific subset of excuses would allow one to cancel a lecture (such as, we assume, the one he is giving). Perhaps for the flu, but most likely not. Perhaps already at this time, Barthes has a cold, or the flu, that will suddenly turn into bronchitis, the fragility and wariness of that extreme period of grief. Potentially for a surgery. Mourning, yes, but society will accept only a limited duration of mourning for an excuse. "Too bad," he writes, "if mourning disorganizes you longer than stated by the code." The right to mourning, he writes curiously, is codified in the same social claims that pregnancy is, but only for a limited time. Weariness, he decides, is an intensity, and society does not allow for intensity. He does not ask not to be weary, but that he is allowed, by society, to luxuriate in his weariness.

Grief is an intensity, exhaustion is an intensity, pregnancy is an intensity—it opens something up, some portal, to meditate on time. Writing grief is writing time. It is about how the past invades the present-tense, the day.

His birthday entry November 12. That a mother is the person you tell things to, he thinks. Sickness. Complaints. You complain to your mother. And how the death of a parent—halts us somehow. For we can be a child, only to our parents.

That I'm now thinking of the Mother in a way I hadn't before. How much I yearn for her, now. Not because I have become a mother, but having become a mother, I have also become again a child. Who needs a mother to complain to, so I do not suffer in silence. And that is what she didn't have. She didn't have a mother to complain to. Before, she was *my* mother, now I think of her too, with a mother, and so on.

And without a mother you have only, I think: a reader.

I didn't understand my mother's suffering until I gave birth. Her specific solitude. What her mornings were like. I tried to imagine. I hadn't lived what it was like to be a mother. Which has added this layer, this new layer of uncanny performance.

How my mother said she would exercise the baby in the morning, set her (me?) on the washing machine. Stretch her arms her legs, make happy noises. As I do this with the baby, a morning ritual, I wonder—was it like this, for her?

Perhaps this is why I do this—it's the one piece of advice, my mother telling me what she'd do when alone with the babies—in her solitude, with us. And then I think of her, having three children under the age of four. How she'd say some days she couldn't brush her teeth. Some days for me too, and I only have one.

I study the minute changes of my baby's pretty sleeping face as my daily meditation. The exquisite pleasure of this.

Why does having a baby make me so more aware of my own mortality? A realization that we were all babies. The absurdity of the photo of Roland Barthes as a baby, in a white dress being held by his mother, that is published in *Mourning Diary*. Cherbourg, 1916. A sleeping blob. His mother Henriette is a young woman, with that look on her face of a mother being photographed with her new baby—attempting to be poised, alert, blissful, bewildered. Another photo. She cradles him in an almost romantic way, he is in her arms, she is stern, protective. His sandy hair and kneesocks. Age seven. Absurd that Roland Barthes was a baby, a child. So absurd for me too—to others but never, ever to myself. The *fact* of my aging.

That return in *Mourning Diary*, the section is divided into "further diary pages" after the first year, as if after a rotation the nature of the diary changes. It does become rare, more sparse, which Barthes feels guilty about, like he should have held on to his suffering, as a form of memory, a form of love. "So forgetting is inexorable (a 'passing sickness'?)."

His rereading of the diary, a return to tears, to emotivity, how it renews mourning, like the first day, how writing, like time, reopens that wound. It is not the suffering that disturbs him, it is the not suffering (the forgetting). Time makes the intensity of mourning pass—and yet, nothing is soothed.

That is writing, in a way: to note that I am still alive. I (the author) at the moment of writing, am still alive. In a way, Roland Barthes is writing every day, "I am still alive."

But when reading *Mourning Diary*, Roland Barthes is not still alive. How mortality is suffused through the text.

He spent a month in the hospital before he died. In the hospital for days without friends knowing he was there, as he was without his identification papers when he was hit by the van. His last manuscript he was working on was an essay about Stendhal entitled, "One Always Fails to Speak of the Things One Loves," left on his desk, unfinished, which I imagine as inspiring the opening Stendhal essay in W. G. Sebald's *Vertigo*.

I read somewhere that those close to him thought that he couldn't fight his injuries, because he was so devastated by his mother's death two years earlier.

It is always the mental arithmetic I do, imagining her age now. We were thirty years apart. She would now be almost 70. On Kawara was 81. Barthes was 64 when he died.

March 17, 2002
July 10, 2014
March 26, 1980

In the hospital for days without people knowing he was there, as he was without his identification papers. (I repeat this because this fact wounds me, with a wirelike sharpness.)

I do not know how On Kawara died. I know how my mother died, because I was there. I do not know how I will die, but I can imagine how much of my work will be unfinished when it happens. Because perhaps the work is always unfinished. But as I write this, and hopefully as you hear this, I am still alive.

Appendix B

WITHHOLDING

AN ERRATA

Sometimes the photograph of a ghost can be discovered by accident. Let me begin with the story of one William Mumler from Boston, a jewelry engraver and amateur photographer who in 1861 discovered in the process of developing a self-portrait the shadow of a young girl looming above his image. Although he knew this was due to the trace of a negative on the same plate, it was recognized by a customer as a distant relative. Aiming to profit on this error, and welcomed by the spiritualist craze at the time, William Mumler realized through *double exposure* he could produce the effect of a ghost relative of an engrieved floating above a customer. There was a trial, and due to various vagaries, an acquittal, and by 1871 he was back in Boston, whereas one Mary Todd Lincoln, in widow's weeds, used the alias of Mrs. Lidall to visit his studio. The resulting photo, with a willowy ghost of Abe Lincoln suspended above her, his long hands planted on her squat shoulders, fingers extended unnaturally like out of an El Greco, was the last photo of Mrs. Lincoln ever taken. The case of William Mumler's duped clients reveals how the photograph

Talk given at Duke University, April 6, 2017

of a ghost, no matter how vague and slippery, can sometimes comfort the surviving—that the dead is still among us, or that the dead can return.

Although I wonder if William Mumler's clients were somehow aware of the hoax, but chose to believe in the fiction of the ghost photograph. It comforted them, thinking this dead loved one was still in the frame, watching them. Yet a photograph of a ghost can also resurrect grief. Roland Barthes's book of photography, *Camera Lucida*, is an elaborate theory that came out of the mourning of his mother, a mourning that was consumptive and total. In *Camera Lucida*, Barthes attempts to answer why one photograph, no matter how vague and slippery, how fragmented the face, can still produce intense emotion in the one still living. In many ways Roland Barthes, like William Mumler, was also developing a self-portrait, although the photograph he was obsessed with was of his mother when she was five years old, standing with her brother, in front of what we are told is a winter garden, or outside greenhouse. At the beginning of *Camera Lucida* he tells us about looking at a photograph of Napoleon's brother, and the thought circulating in him, that of the *gaze*—that here were the eyes that stared at the emperor. A shiver to realize this, of history's shadows. Perhaps when he is writing this he is already thinking of this Winter Garden photograph, the exact image he chooses to withhold from us in *Camera Lucida*, thinking of his mother's brother, and how his mother's brother gazed at his mother when she was a child, and thus knew some secret or mystery about his mother that now never can be revealed. In *Camera Lucida*, Roland Barthes fixates on photographs of children, thinking of this one ghost photograph. There is something, he decides, palpably sad, about the photograph of a child from another era. The ghostliness of such an image—the photographed young have their whole lives ahead of them, and also, they are already dead. There is a twinning in a photograph, a double exposure, the future floating into the frame of a seemingly fixed past. Both a "certificate of presence," as Barthes writes, and also irreparably about absence. He writes of "that rather terrible thing which is there in every photograph: *the return of the dead.*"

THE WINTER GARDEN

I would like to think through the decision Roland Barthes makes to withhold the actual photograph of his mother in the Winter Garden from *Camera Lucida*, his book which was published just before his accidental death, hit by a laundry van crossing the streets of Paris after lunch with the future president of France. Barthes's various decisions to withhold, in this case the photograph, in other examples, more revealing details of his autobiography, have always fascinated me. He is the thinker I think through now. I am most interested in how he chooses to live and think through his mourning, the two years following his mother's death, which also became the last two years remaining of his life. I am interested in thinking of mourning as a period that is potentially rich and verdant. I am also interested in thinking of writing as following after ghosts.

I've thought through this decision before, his decision to withhold the photograph, in the book I wrote about my mother, which is also a book of photography and ghosts. But still it interests me. In some ways this decision to withhold the photograph is a protective gesture on the part of the mourning son. That there needs to still be privacy in mourning. He writes that it wouldn't produce the same effect on the reader to show us the image. All we would be able to do, at best, is notice certain details—what clothes the two young children are wearing, indicative of the time period, perhaps their expressions, and meditate on their youth or mortality in the most general way, like Barthes looking and thinking about other photographs in *Camera Lucida*. Perhaps we would, like the photograph of Napoleon's brother, think—Ah! these are the eyes that gazed at the philosopher! But there would be distance, and for Roland Barthes, there is no distance. He maintains throughout that he is not interested in the one taking the photographs, he is not even an amateur photographer, he is actually somewhat bored by photographs as works of art. He chooses not to illustrate the text with the photograph, leaving instead a space of absence for us to consider. There would be no wound for us, he writes, if he did allow us to look upon her face, which he names the *punctum* of a photograph. The Winter Garden photograph is a ghost for us partially because we do not see it.

It is likely Roland Barthes came upon this Winter Garden photograph after his mother's death, while going through the mundane ritual of flipping through the albums, in their shared apartment, or perhaps these photographs were not housed in an album, but loose within a box of photographs. I don't know what kind of cataloguer Henriette Barthes was. It seems that the existence of the photograph is something of an event for him, so it's not an image that he would have known or registered before (a sign of age: to study photographs from before we were born). Most of the photographs he flips through do not cause him pain. He does not love them. He does, later, have the Winter Garden photograph framed. It hangs above his writing desk in a triptych of three framed photographs. The other photographs are of the house at Urt, where they summered, and which he returns to, after her death, with such agony, and then also a photograph of camels in Morocco where he holidayed after his mother died, finding that being away actually increased his mourning. I learn of this triptych of photographs in his posthumously published *Mourning Diary* and see them reproduced in a photograph of his study. I only know that one of the framed pictures is the mythical Winter Garden photograph because of the caption, but it is too grainy for me to see. I do wonder whether he would have been happy to have the Winter Garden photograph duplicated, in any way, along with the other family photos reproduced in *Mourning Diary*, as this seems counter to the project of withholding and absence in *Camera Lucida*.

Roland Barthes must write an entire book to figure out why it is that this Winter Garden photograph produces such *punctum*. Is it the small, tender detail, he wonders, or an overall intensity? It obsesses him with, he writes, in a phrase that I love, "a kind of vertigo, something of a 'detective anguish'." This tells me too that the impact of this particular photograph came upon its discovery, that he could not ask his mother about it when she was alive. He writes that the Winter Garden Photograph, as he capitalizes it, is his Ariadne, "not because it would help me discover a secret thing (monster or treasure), but because it would tell me what constituted that thread which drew me towards Photography." In Greek myth Ariadne gives Theseus the ball of red thread to escape from the labyrinth and kill the Minotaur. Ariadne is the daughter of the King and Queen of Crete, and later, is the bride of Dionysus. But when I think of Ariadne with her red thread I think as well of the Maman spider sculptures of Louise Bourgeois, and her red spools of thread in her Cells, symbolizing her mother the weaver of tapestries. Roland Barthes continues with this maternal metaphor of the photograph: "A sort of umbilical cord links the body of the photographed thing to my gaze..."

A photograph does not bring back a memory of the past, he muses. It is not Proustian (he is reading everything through Proust in this period of later work). It does announce, mechanically, that this event or person once existed. It is a confirmation of existence, always a copy, never the original. It is a form of resurrection, he notes, bringing up the image of Christ which appears on Veronica's veil, once she wiped his bleeding and sweating face with it. A portrait, a sort of monoprint, a precursor to the first photograph. And yet the image of Christ appears before an unnamed stranger, a miracle. Roland Barthes is more interested in the iconography of mother and son. He seems to suggest, somehow, that the true *punctum* of the photo of his mother as a child is his own mortality as well as hers— she is a child, she will die, she has died; I was a child, I will die.

A VISITATION

Recently when I've been staring at my daughter's sleeping face I have felt an uncanny feeling—like I am staring at myself as a baby, or my sister's face as a baby, as my baby is more fair than I am and more like my sister. The feeling is unsettling, but in a calm way. Perhaps it is unsettling because it makes me feel somehow I am resurrected as my mother, that if I am gazing at myself as a baby or my sister, then I am my mother, or I see in some ways what she did, the faces she made her meditation. Every morning now my baby's face looks different. Every day her eyes look a bit closer together, or perhaps further apart. We think her eyes might be green, although sometimes they look blue. I take photos of her every day, as she gazes at me. Will the photographs later reveal the nuances, the gradation? Her face a changing timeline.

I asked my father, when he recently visited, to bring a photograph of myself as a baby. My father brings me two large photo albums in a black duffel bag. He presents them to me, in the black duffel bag, and immediately wants me to go make copies of the ones I want, as he's protective of the family photographs and is uneasy to let them out of his sight. After my mother's death, over a decade ago, my father let us make copies of our childhood photographs, not wanting to part with the originals, even though a photograph is never an original, it is always a copy. I made copies of the most beautiful, dreamy photographs of my mother as a young woman and of me as a child, that I then stored in a box. To think of copying a photograph reminds me of the processes W. G. Sebald underwent to make the found photographs in his narratives look aged, how he would photocopy them over and over again, to make them look fuzzy, dreamlike. I don't look at these photographs, but remember them, in this fuzzy, dreamlike way, that is still painful, but almost painful as if through a gauzy filter, because I don't look at them directly. I have written about them in a book, which being published, is now stored away as well, like in a box, which I won't take out and look at anymore.

Like Roland Barthes's wrangling over the surprise of emotions in the Winter Garden photograph, I would like to understand why these twin albums of photographs, whose existence I was unaware of, stirred and disturbed me so utterly. I was in a mood all weekend, brought about by these images and my father's visit, a mood of sadness and rage. Perhaps I can describe the albums in which the photographs are housed. They are of a cheap scalloped blue and white design. These photographs were once stored in boxes in the living room cabinet, and in stuffed yellow drugstore envelopes. There were also other photo albums, the leather-bound ones my mother catalogued. These were not those photographs. My mother's scrapbook placed each photograph in a specific narrative and time, on the page. My father's album is defined by its refusal to condense and its haphazardness.

To go through a photo album is to move back through time. The first album begins with my father's scrawled handwriting. My mother's apartment, probably the summer of 1975, he notes. Two identical photos of my pigtailed half-sister, my mother's daughter, at five years old, standing in front of a card table. My mother slim in a sweater stands in front of a white cake at her wedding shower, candles lit on the table.

I slide these images out of the plastic, yet I cannot see them any clearer. I study the honeymoon photos in Hawaii. A dim succession of aerial landscapes, like badly produced postcards, absent of people, taken from a skyscraper hotel, I assume. I am struck by their emptiness. One of the photographs from Hawaii is loose in the album, depicting my mother in a short green halter dress, standing in front of a fence, my father's thumb in half the frame.

It obsesses me, and infuriates me, this finger, this ghostly smudge. Roland Barthes writes that the photograph's *punctum* is the accident, its error. "A photograph's *punctum* is that accident which pricks me (but also bruises me, is poignant to me.)" Many of these photographs are both out of focus and have become sepia-toned through time. These indifferent assembly-line drugstore-developed productions. My father didn't see the photographs when he put them in the album, didn't notice that there were doubles, twins.

Photographs of various parties or weddings, then photographs of my older half-sister as a child, her birthdays. Then the move through time: my other sister being born, me being born, my brother, our birthdays, Christmases, and times at the cabin. The incredibly sad narrative that emerges. My half-sister, special, singular, then fading away, in the background, when there are new babies. She disappears from the second album, becomes the ghost. I don't know why I have such a need to catalogue this, to archive it into language. I doubt that it is interesting to others, except perhaps the feeling underneath it.

The photos are stuffed in, hurriedly. My father has confused the chronology. I can chart my changing face. The second album continues on the same day the last one ended, the Christmas when I am one year old. The night I first studied these albums, I began to sob, violently, and could not stop. I still don't understand why. Perhaps me on my uncle's lap, my uncle, my father's identical twin, who is no longer alive. Me with my dolly. My white tights and diapers clinging to my pretty mother days later on my birthday, my mother in her orange turtleneck and gold necklaces lifting me up, my ruffled cloth diaper. The photos up at the cabin. My plaid ruffled overalls. My grandmother dressed my sister and me as twins, which my mother disliked. We were only a year apart. Me as a baby on my grandmother's lap. My uncle's hand on my head. My sister's and my footied pajamas.

My father is the amateur photographer in most of these. There's no care to the framing or lighting, no apparent attempt to see the object being photographed in these images. The first day he was over he immediately pulled out his tiny digital camera and said he needed a photograph of him with his granddaughter "before she decides she doesn't like me." It's not that babies don't like you, I tried to explain, it's that they get uncomfortable having to sit still for too long. I tried to suggest that he simply enjoy her, why not look at her face, why this need to take a photograph? But I placed her on his lap and we tried to take photographs with his dingy camera, tried to turn the flash off. It died almost immediately, having run out of batteries. We took a series of photos with one of our phones. He still wanted to make a print—a 7 by 11 of one from his camera to put in a frame.

When she turns one, he says to me, you have to go get a professional photograph of her to put on my wall of grandchildren. I will not, I said, dress her in a dress and take her to get a studio photograph where she has to pose stiffly. This made me think of Walter Benjamin writing of the two studio photographs of Kafka as a child in "The Lamp," a sketch for his Berlin childhood memoir, confusing it in such a slippery way with his own memories of being photographed. The sadness and shame he sees in little Franz K's face, the melancholy of the commercial studio portrait. In writing "The Lamp," Benjamin becomes Kafka, merging the ghostly memory of his childhood with these photographs of Kafka.

Last night flipping through the album, I became aware of how much time has passed, and how the majority of the elders are not alive anymore. In these chaotic and happy scenes of family— bustling, brimming, so many toys littering every room, the kitchens, I'm surprised how messy it all is—I sense the solitude of everyone's death, my mother's, my uncle's, and, someday, my own. How close birth is to death. It's stupid to say this. It is what cannot be communicated but only felt, in a photo. That these were photos of ghosts. How I have avoided, for years, looking at photographs of my childhood, these photographs that my mother curated, chose, framed...how beautiful I found these photographs, I imbued them with all the innocence and sentimentality of my youth. The passage of time is the *punctum*—I understand it now, it is the overall effect, that I was a baby, gazing at my mother the way my baby gazes at me, and that I will die.

I stop to take a series of photographs on my phone of John and the baby. She is wiggling on his lap, he is humming to her, they are at ease, moving together, trying to not make too much noise so I can write. I take constant photographs of the baby, of me, of me with the baby, of the baby with her father, of me breastfeeding the baby, of the baby and the dog, of me and the dog. This constant, casual, documentation. Perhaps I wish to remember something of how this felt, of the life of the thing. How to record the shifts of her darling face. A mournfulness that can suffocate me. The energy of my baby. How I cannot believe four months have passed. She doesn't understand yet what it means to stare at a screen, mirroring herself to get her photo taken. But she's interested in mirrors. In staring at faces, in studying expressions. My phone urges me to make a slideshow of the photos I've taken backed by a menu of possible canned Muzak: Gentle, Dreamy, Sentimental, Happy, Epic, Club.

Perhaps I have already said too much about the contents of these photo albums. There is no bruise, no wound, for you.

I often wonder how much I should withhold in writing. I especially agonized over this in the book about my mother. There are many descriptions of photographs of my mother in that book, but only one photograph of her is reproduced in the book, along with a still of Barbara Loden from her 1971 film *Wanda*. I was struck by how both the actress and my mother were posed in profile in such similar ways in the same time period, both partially obscured by a parked car in the foreground, which interrupts the frame. Struck by the ghostliness of this double exposure. Someone I know, a well-known novelist, when she read the book in galley, wrote to me that I must not use the photograph of my mother, that this was a mistake. She wrote that in reading the book, she created in her mind a projection of what my mother looked like, and it hurt the effect to be met with her face. At this point, it was far too late for me to have changed anything, as the book was already at the printer, and I would have chosen to keep the diptych of photos in anyway. But I wrote her that I found this interesting (if unrequited) feedback, and perhaps I was wrong, perhaps I should have withheld the photograph, perhaps this was an error. For me, it was less that it illustrated what she looked like, as a young woman, but was more a photograph that had a cinematic blankness, much like Barbara Loden's *Wanda*, a film based on a newspaper clipping of a real-life woman who fell into becoming an accomplice in a bank robbery. The photograph in this case opened up a space of absence to meditate upon. My mother as a mystery, as an actress, like a film still. When I wrote her back, I mentioned to her the moment in W. G. Sebald's *Austerlitz* where the reader finally sees the image of Jacques Austerlitz as a child, the found photograph, found both by Jacques Austerlitz and found by Sebald and fictionalized as authentic. How this is a moment in the text that is somehow a shock, coming so late in the book. The beautiful sadness of the blonde boy in the field, dressed in costume as a page for his mother's Rose Queen.

I wanted to think more about this, about Sebald's *Austerlitz*, a novel which was inspired by a deep reading of Roland Barthes's *Camera Lucida*. I wanted to think more about the photograph of the mother as a ghost, and of accident or error. In *Austerlitz*, the unnamed Sebald stand-in learns the life story of an architectural historian named Jacques Austerlitz, who grew up raised by a preacher and his wife in Wales but learned that he was born in Prague and sent to Wales as part of a children's transport during the war, and that his parents, whose memory he had repressed, had died in the camps. Over several episodes, over many decades, meeting almost always accidentally, Jacques Austerlitz tells the narrator his newly discovered life story. The narrator then writes down his narrative, "in the form of notes and disconnected sentences."

Sebald was an inventor of ghosts, visualized in the found photographs he used in his narratives. Once Jacques Austerlitz discovers the hallucinations of his childhood to be true, he searches for a photograph of his mother. One day his Prague nanny, who has told him the story of his origins, says that she found two photographs that slipped out when she began reading a red leather-bound edition of Balzac. One of these photographs turns out to be a hoax of sorts— it is of an Alpine stage set, with a man and a woman, seen almost in miniature, who turn out not to be Jacques Austerlitz's parents. The other is the photo of Jacques Austerlitz as a five-year-old boy staring at the camera dressed as the page of the Snow Queen, who is his mother, and annotated in Czech by his grandfather's hand.

In the edition of *Austerlitz* that I have there is an error in the text at this moment, right as Vera, Austerlitz's former nanny and now an old woman, discovers the two loose photographs, of mysterious provenance, in a volume of Balzac, and hands them to Austerlitz, who then curiously, we are told, hands them to the narrator, along with the other collection of photographs scattered through the text, apparently for safekeeping. On page 181 of my 2001 Modern Library edition, published the year that Sebald died in a car accident, it reads "with every breath we   two small photographs measuring about three by four inches from the little occasional table besides her chair." There is a double space where a word is missing, which I originally thought was "took," as in "with every breath we took," but a search on Google Books of the 2002 edition reveals that the missing word is "drew," "with every breath we drew." Before going to Google Books I had examined my other, identical copy of *Austerlitz*, the one that is not underlined on every page, and found the same error. For some time, on the couch, the two copies of *Austerlitz* sat together, with the photo of Jacques Austerlitz as a little page boy on the cover side by side like haunting blonde twins.

After realizing that the small indistinct woman in the Alpine stage set is a fake, or at least not his mother, Jacques Austerlitz is seized with this detective anguish, this vertigo, to find the original version of his mother, the actress, not a fake or copy, much like Jimmy Stewart in the Hitchcock film searches after Madeleine, who he sees as the original, the woman he fell in love with, the woman he thought was haunted by a ghost in a painting, but who turns out to be played by an actress, a copy, a hoax.

There are several hoaxes, in which Jacques Austerlitz thinks he might have glimpsed a ghost of his mother, and chooses to suspend his disbelief, just like the suffering customers of William Mumler, who wanted to believe that the shadow of a relative suspended above them in the photograph was real, and not fictionalized. Ever the historian, Austerlitz searches for any visual documentation of his mother in various archives. Through a history of the Theresienstadt camp, where his mother was sent, he learns of the existence of a propaganda film on the camp that was filmed for the Red Cross. By searching through various archives, he finally is able to watch a VHS copy of the film, which turns out to contain only an opening sequence, a patchwork of scenes cobbled together, totaling fourteen minutes. He plays the tape over and over in an attempt to catch his mother somewhere in the frame. He even gets a slow-motion copy of this fragment made, which reminds me of Joseph Cornell splicing scenes from *East of Borneo* into the collage film *Rose Hobart*, focusing exclusively on his actress, the object of his obsession, a film now totaling nineteen minutes. As Sebald writes, and Austerlitz narrates, what emerges is a dream film, in which the men and women in the workshops look like they are sleepwalking, another film altogether, much like the silent *Rose Hobart* emerges as another film altogether from the Universal adventure film that is its source.

The way the outlines of the actors' bodies seem to be dissolved at the edges reminds Austerlitz, Sebald writes, of "the frayed outlines of the human hand shown in the fluidal pictures and electrographs taken by Louis Draget in Paris around the turn of the century." As

I am rereading and slowing down this passage of Sebald's, I notice another error. In this passage, Sebald is referencing the fluidal pictures of one Louis Darget, spelled incorrectly in the text, an early example of spirit photography. Darget theorized that by placing a plate over one's forehead one could photograph someone's thoughts or dreams, in this case that of his wife's. The electrograph hand Sebald is referencing, through Austerlitz's narration, is almost certainly not Darget's but the famous early X-ray taken by Wilhelm Conrad Röntgen. An X-ray from 1896 of the hand of his wife, who upon seeing her frayed fuzzy hand as a photograph, remarked, "I have seen my own death."

Roland Barthes also wishes to make a slow-motion fragment of his mother in the Winter Garden photograph. Like Austerlitz lingering over this still of his non-mother, a copy-mother, a ghost mother, Sebald wishes to enlarge the image of his mother's face as a child, in order to see it better. "I decompose, I enlarge, and so to speak, I *retard*, in order to have time to *know* at last." Like Muybridge's photos of bodies in motion, but to enlarge it, to slow down, to make it like a trance film—as Austerlitz actually does.

Perhaps this is what I wished to do with this still of my mother lingering before a car. I wished to make her a film still. I wished to gaze at her face. My mother an actress, as a young woman she is a fiction, everything that she has withheld, that she still withholds, in her death. A photograph is a temporal hallucination, Barthes writes. She has been renamed and remade. Later Jacques Austerlitz will come across the headshot of an actress in the Prague theatrical archives who slightly resembled the woman he remembered as his mother, and that is the photograph that stands in for the mother, fiction or ghost. Jacques Austerlitz gazes at the face of this actress in the still, and sees in her face something like the resemblance of the shadowy mother of his reawakened memories.

GOODNIGHT NOBODY

I wish to slow down this writing of the photograph of the ghost mother. I would like it to be still. Barthes notes that the Latin *punctum* shares the same root as *punctuation*, which makes me think of the spaces in between, the blanks. Marguerite Duras who writes of her childhood in *The Lover* as a blank space, an over-exposed photograph. "The story of my childhood does not exist," she writes. "Does not exist," she repeats. She has written these same scenes of her childhood, but before, they were rendered clearly, in the light. Now she wishes to repeat again, to go back, and write of the ghosts of that same youth, to what is buried. This is the writing of the *punctum* of the photograph—that which is too vague, faded, that which we cannot see.

What does it mean to write a ghost? What form does it take?

When extremely sleep deprived you can become convinced that you are a ghost. There is a disintegration of language and time. My daughter is still not sleeping much at night, so we are superstitious during the day about her naps. It is like we are sleepwalking through the day, tiptoeing around with the blinds drawn and the lights down low. We put on the music all day long, its loops and repetitions, which reminds me of the music I would play on repeat when writing the mother book. At night, to establish ritual, I read her *Goodnight*

Moon. She cannot quite sit still through all of it. I want to read it slowly, with the inflection of the night, of fatigue, to lull her to sleep. But for now, I have to read it to her at a quicker tempo, so she can tolerate it.

In *Goodnight Moon* the little bunny in a great green room must say good night to many fanciful and everyday objects—a red balloon, a telephone, a mouse, a little house, a comb, a pair of framed nursery rhyme scenarios, while the old lady rocks and knits in her rocking chair. We say goodnight to the room, the framed pictures, the red balloon, etc. There is a moment that startles me every time. A page, otherwise blank, that reads only "Goodnight nobody." The facing page is "Goodnight mush" with its accompanying illustration (to rhyme with the previous brush). Goodnight nobody. I think about this page a lot, this strange existential punctuation in the midst of what is supposed to be a calming children's book.

We are told that the bigger bunny in the apron in the rocking chair is the "quiet old lady whispering hush." Examining the scenario, it makes more sense that she is the mother, or perhaps the grandmother. Then why is she referred to as the "quiet old lady"? She is also a bunny, they are the same species but anthropomorphized, unlike the kittens and the mouse playing on the carpet.

Who is speaking to whom? I notice, upon further reads, that earlier there is no grandmother bunny, just the ball of string and green yarn on an empty chair. Later, she appears. So is she a ghost? Inside the room I also notice there is a framed rendering of a big bunny, with a baby bunny, but it's grainier, in black and white, like a memory.

The *punctum* is a tiny fragment or dot. What does that look like in a text? Can a text be pricked? Perhaps the writing of the ghost mother, which is the ghost childhood, must necessarily be fragmented. Intercut with blanks, providing a break in the text. A mark or wound. The elliptical fragments of Nathalie Sarraute's memoir, *Childhood*, conjures this. "I want to touch, to caress this immutable image, to cover it with words, but not too thickly, I'm so afraid of spoiling it…"A childhood in Russia, then her emigration with her mother to Paris. The hallucinations of early memories, childhood as a fever dream, like Jacques Austerlitz suffering from aphasia, his inability to find language for his memories. She wakes up and sees her mother in her pince-nez, reading a book, while she sleeps, just like the old lady / bunny / ghost in *Goodnight Moon*.

GHOST IMAGE

In the title piece of his book on photography, *Ghost Image*, Hervé Guibert narrates being a teenager and wanting to take a photograph of his mother, whose fragile beauty he sees as fading once she enters middle age. She is one of those women, he writes, who fancies herself to resemble a certain actress. Usually his mother refuses to be photographed (like my mother refused to be photographed), resisting the constant photography of his father, an amateur photographer with his own developing equipment. The young Hervé shuts his father out from the room. He takes his mother and washes her face, does her hair and her face exactly as he wishes. He puts her in front of natural, beautiful light, and takes her photograph. Only later, he realizes, that the entire roll of film was ruined, an accident. "But I had to confront the evidence: I hadn't completely attached the film in the camera…It had slipped off the small black teeth that held it in place and advanced, and I had photographed nothing."

The illustrations for this text, he writes, can only be a piece of blank film. If the picture had existed, he would not have had to write this text. The process of writing replaces that of photography. Writing is essentially, Guibert writes, ghostly, a melancholy act.

"For this text is the despair of the image, and worse than a blurred or fogged image—a ghost image…" The ghost image—the image that doesn't exist, that's really what we write towards, that memory.

Appendix C

TRANSLATIONS OF THE UNCANNY

I.

Recently the writer Sofia Samatar and I have been engaged in an ongoing conversation on literature and the uncanny. These conversations take place over email, as we send each other scraps of our readings, descriptions of untranslated texts that we wish to read, Internet research tangents, pirated PDFs of theory books, notes and meditations that we are free to borrow or steal from. These investigations are sometimes punctuated by notes on the drama of domesticity, my new baby, considering various academic invitations, complaints about the invisibility of our new books, or the nature of their visibility, the alienating or non-event publishing can feel like. Sometimes we find ourselves reading the identical text at the same exact time, and this discovery has ceased to surprise us. I am never surprised, upon picking up, for instance, Roberto Bolaño's *Antwerp*, to know that Sofia is reading it simultaneously, without either of us mentioning the title yet to each other. I knew however when I mentioned to Sofia I was thinking of writing an appendix on "definitions or translations of

Talk given on May 11, 2017 at The Renaissance Society at the University of Chicago for the B. Ingrid Olson and Astrid Klein exhibit the uncanny" that this was one of her primary fields of research, being a writer and thinker immersed in the ghostly and speculative, and I could only glean from her wisdom. But I did not realize that her interest in the strange and uncertain sensation that we call in English the "uncanny" had encompassed lately not only the idea of the double or notions of reoccurrence, but also particularly the question of space. We are both writing about space and the uncanny, at the same time, it turns out, which does not surprise us. This month Sofia has been working on an article on the Sudanese writer Tayeb Salih, in which she examines the uncanniness of intertextuality—like the moment in his novel *Season of Migration to the North*, when the narrator's double begins speaking in perfect English in the middle of a square. As for me, I am simply working on these talks, that are like a series of footnotes or asides, which attempt to reconsider the various errata and omissions of the book I have just published. Sofia tells me about a book entitled *The Author and His Doubles*, which circles around classical Arabic literary modes, and concepts of copying, plagiarism, misattribution, and "disappearing and mislaid authors," she writes. In the classical period, a writer could gift a poem to someone else, and it could be published under someone else's name.[1] Sofia knows this would interest me, as so much of our ongoing conversation over the past year and a half has dealt with varieties of literary disappearance, in the mode of Henri Lefebvre's *The Missing Pieces*, Enrique Vila-Matas's *Bartleby & Co*, and the writers that haunt W. G. Sebald. She is interested, she writes me, in "abjection and self-immolation of a literary kind," which interests me too, as she well knows:

---

1. I wonder, then, if it's possible, if Sofia could write this talk for me, and I could publish it under my name. Although even if this were to happen, how would anyone know?

(52)

the performance of disappearance, the poetics of anonymity. I tell her about my desire to not even publish these appendices, or to publish them in some almost invisible way without an ISBN, and she writes me recently of her dream of publishing a book, under no name, and distributing it freely in public spaces, like train station bathrooms.[2] And yet I think we are also aware that simultaneous to this shared fantasy of anonymity, our Pessoa fantasies, we also complain that we have books out now and no one's reading them, we are not on most of the lists, always this tension between a desire for invisibility and worrying over our own ghostliness. For both of us, it is not the visible remnants of the texts we are working on that interest us, these are just the remaining fragments of the larger works we haven't written yet, the speculative, possible, yet quixotic, work. Currently, I am working on a series about literature and disappearance that has yet to materialize, which exists in an archive of various notebooks and boxed drafts and various passionate Gmail chains. This journal article Sofia is now writing is but a fragment of a six-book series on literary decadence and dissolution she hopes to write, the research for which is vast and ongoing. Simultaneously with writing this academic article she is collecting notes and quotes for one of the books she's planning in the series, a book on Edgar Allen Poe, and thinking of how she will translate this article from the academic language in which she's now writing it, into yet another book, these potential projects endlessly multiplying so that everything we think about we turn somehow into a potential book, our possible infinite and invisible library. For us

2. When I send Sofia this talk, she remarks that that morning, in fact, she had mused that the final section of this novel she would never write would be called *Argentina*, "as a sort of sideways nod to *Antwerp*, and a wink toward Knausgaard, who said in an interview that he thought of calling his series *Argentina* instead due to his love of Argentine writers, and of course, as an homage to Borges."

there's so much potential and energy in a project that is unfinished, so much to dream into, within all of our notes all the infinite possibility of literature, that is deflated by the actual books and the process of publishing. Or, beyond the question of publishing, our actual writing feels a shadow of what we could have written, and so it is in our next book that we can truly transcend. In this way, I think, we both are performing shadow versions of Borges's Symbolist poet Pierre Menard's absurd heroism—the desire, not to write a contemporary version of *Don Quixote*, not to simply translate it into another language, but to somehow give birth to an identical text, yet possible only in fragments. I have been complaining to Sofia about this project of the appendix I've chosen to take on, how unnecessary and tangential these texts feel, how agonizing it has been to make the time during this period where I am so consumed, with everything about the baby, constant nursing and her recent separation anxiety, so that everything else in my life, teaching and writing et cetera feels rushed and done in the available pockets of the day. That I work on these appendices, which have been taking the form of talks, in the edges and corners of everything else. And still I'm compelled to keep on circling back to my failures and errata in my attempt at writing this now published book. Sofia is of course enthused about the unnecessary, the extraneous, what has been erased.[3] Also: perhaps

---

3. Sofia writes me:

"Which is what the appendices seem like—like an afterbirth. Some kind of placenta which is, like the appendix, no longer necessary, extra.

What to do with the extra?

It's a way of continuing past the end. That's where the question 'what to do with the appendices' becomes so compelling, philosophically. Why go past the end? But I think we know, without being able to answer precisely, that there is something very alive and incandescent and yes, richly uncanny, about these leftovers."

an appendix as a form is uncanny, a doubling and return back to a previous text.

I keep on rereading Freud's essay on "The Uncanny," or rather, his essay on *"Das Unheimliche,"* which is translated into the English as "The Uncanny," even though this is not the exact equivalent, of course, but a weird double who functions enough like the original. In the final form of *Book of Mutter*, I excised a passage where I attempted an etymology of the uncanny, or *unheimlich*, connecting it to its root of *heim*, or home. Although I altered and attempted to correct the passage over several different drafts, as I can see on my desktop, the draft from 2013 differing subtly from that from 2016, when I finally excised the passage. Over these many drafts over several years, I consulted two German translators of my acquaintance, who both told me that my translation of the uncanny, as I situated it within the mother's house and in the concept of space, wasn't accurate or correct, and so fearing, as always, stupidity, or graduate students writing me of my error, I reactively excised it, although felt compelled enough by this question of translation and space that I kept on returning to it, and altering and adapting it, over the course of several years. In the passage's final published form, I use the word "uncanny," to try to put a word to the strange sensation of feeling my mother as a ghostly presence immediately after her death, as I returned to live with my father in my childhood home, me mimicking her movements, as I folded balding towels. The nervous sensation I was attempting to describe was not only of the body (me being her mirror and double) but also of the house, feeling the house as this vast, ghostly, space. Which reminds me of a passage in Leonora Carrington's *The Hearing Trumpet*, that I recently read and wrote down: "Houses are really bodies. We connect ourselves with walls, roofs, and objects just as we hang on to our livers, skeletons, flesh and bloodstream." This also recalls Louise Bourgeois's paintings of the *Femme Maison* series, the women with houses for heads, a visual pun that I conjure up in the book. After using the phrase "uncanny," I then attempted, briefly, to locate the translation of *unheimliche* into English as being not only uncanny, but also ghostly, or (of a house) haunted, which is correct. Three years later, in 2016, I went further, into what was previously a cursory reading of Freud's essay, and wrote that the primary definition for the antonym for *unheimlich*, or *heimlich*, is "cozy or familiar," but a more arcane definition of *heimlich* is "concealed, secret, private," so that the concept of home is tied up with the concept of what is hidden.

The thing is, I realize now, I was not wrong, in my reading of Freud's essay on strangeness and uncertainty, which contains in its first part his extensive etymology of *unheimliche* in German and English. Perhaps I should not have excised the passage so easily, or tortured it under this rhythm of disappearing and emergence. Sofia wrote this to me as well, when I originally told her I was thinking of writing an appendix entitled "Translations of the Uncanny," about this excised passage that now exists in the invisible digital archive. Freud's own essay, she wrote to me, is so experimental and unsure, how could these German translators be so certain, when his essay is actually about uncertainty? I read through the emails with one of my translator friends, a writer living in Spain who has translated the first, novella-length book of Marianne Fritz's magnum opus, an Austrian writer whose work is described as untranslatable, and he pointed me to the vagueness of an exact etymology within the *heim* entry in Grimm's dictionary.

Of course, this led me last week on to another unnecessary research tangent on the Grimm brothers, who were near but not exact twins, and how one married and the other didn't, but they both lived with the one's wife, and how they set about this extensive and passionate enterprise of an exhaustive German dictionary, all while being exiled from various academic environments and cities because of the political climate, while still continuing this slow task. They left the dictionary unfinished, after one died, and the other mourned, and the project was only finished long after their death. I remember that the final entry of the last brother was *Fruchte*, or Fruit, which I found an appealing anecdote that I'd store to use later.

II.

When I was writing the book on my mother, over those years, I felt that since the etymology was uncertain, I should excise my passage. However, I now realize that the uncanny is an ambivalent space, and so is Freud's text on it. "What makes space uncanny—the mother's house—and how is the uncanny itself, the term, a space?" Sofia writes to me, encouraging me. And so I have felt again compelled to return to this space of the uncanny, much like Freud returned to his essay on the uncanny, after years of putting it away in a drawer, much like my book itself was in a drawer, for years, such as in the gap between 2013 and 2016. I attempt to trace through the uncertain movements of Freud's essay, reading it side by side with Hélène Cixous's essay "Fictions and its Phantoms," in which she produces a close reading of Freud's essay that she wonderfully describes as a "strange theoretical novel." Cixous's close reading of Freud mirrors

Freud's close reading of E.T.A Hoffman's "The Sandman" in the second section of "The Uncanny." The space of Freud's essay is itself a labyrinth, as Cixous writes, as he wanders uncertainly and ambivalently through his reading of the uncanny. He sets about in the essay to disprove an originary essay on the psychology of the uncanny, that uncanniness comes from uncertainty in real-life. The space of the word *uncanny*, an unsettling word in its uncertainty, an uncertain reading, a sort of vertiginous movement that Freud traces, which returns back to itself. Ultimately in this first part he shows that what is familiar and intimate, what is of the house, collapses into its opposite, the strange, the unfamiliar, the haunted. "For us the most interesting fact to emerge from this long excerpt is that among the various shades of meaning that are recorded for the word *Heimlich* there is one in which it merges with its formal antonym, *unheimlich*, so that what is called *Heimlich* becomes *unheimlich*."

Sofia writes to me that the only mention of space she can think of in Freud's essay on the uncanny is the passage in the red-light district, which is Freud's attempt to illuminate the repetition of the same thing, this other phenomenon that can initiate an uncanny sensation. In a rare first-person aside, Freud remembers wandering around the empty and unfamiliar streets of an Italian town, in what feels like a dream, repeatedly getting lost, until finding himself in a red-light district, which he kept on returning to, like in a maze or labyrinth, which seized him with an anxious feeling. On this same page, where the reader as Cixous describes gets lost on "the corner of some street or paragraph," Freud compares that same unsettling feeling with groping around a dark, unfamiliar room and colliding with the same piece of furniture. When reading this, I think about the first story in Borges's *Labyrinths*, the Borges narrator's discovery of the province

Uqbar with Adolfo Bioy Casares, one night at dinner, through an encyclopedia and a mirror: "The mirror troubled the depths of a corridor in a country house…" I read a set of interviews with Borges in Indiana at the age of 80, a passage I then send to Sofia: "I always stood in fear of mirrors. When I was a little boy, there was something awful at my house. In my room we had three full-length mirrors. Then also the furniture was of mahogany, and that made a kind of dark mirror, like the mirrors to be found in Saint Paul's epistle. I stood in fear of them, but being a child I did not dare say anything. So every night I was confronted by three or four images of myself. I felt that to be really awful." When writing my book of the mother, I wanted to think of the text like a house, maybe a haunted house. In the book on my mother, I thought of Louise Bourgeois's Cells as well, her salvaged architectural spaces, filled with mirrors, her sculptures, clothing and objects, these sites of psychoanalytic dread and anxiety, of the childhood home. Could each paragraph or page be like moving into a series of rooms, refracted and reflected with mirrors, getting lost, constantly returning?

Two other strange punctures of the first-person in Freud's essay: an aside in which he tells us that he was flipping through a pulp magazine and read a horror story that he found poorly written yet unsettling, thinking through literature as the most ideal country of the uncanny. Also, in a footnote to his writing on the uncanny effect of the double, Freud remembers being in the sleeping compartment of a train, when the mirrored door of the adjacent toilet swings open, as the train lurches, and Freud is surprised to see an elderly man in a dressing gown and a cap staring at him, only to finally piece together that the intruder was in fact his own image reflected in a mirror, an anecdote itself mirroring one found in a book by an

E. Mach. "I can still recall that I found his appearance thoroughly unpleasant," Freud writes. "Hence, instead of being frightened by our 'doubles,' both Mach and I simply failed to recognize them. Or was the displeasure we felt at seeing these unexpected images of ourselves perhaps a vestige of the archaic reaction to the 'double' as something uncanny?"[4]

III.

It makes sense that the third part, and final section, of this talk, mirroring Freud's three-part meditation on strangeness and uncertainty, would be thinking through doubling and space and the work of two artists whose works are so occupied with layers, text, perception, and ambivalence. It makes sense because Freud's essay on the uncanny is, as he announces in the first line, an "aesthetic investigation," extending off of Edmund Burke's work on the sublime, thinking through this specific class of the frightening, work that is strange and filled with anxiety. I like the idea of thinking about art that produces weird and uncertain sensations,

---

4. What leaps out to me, Sofia writes me, when she reads this talk: the word "vestige," like a vestigial, unexpected feeling, a pain in the gut like an appendix, something archaic, she writes. And I realize, when she writes me this, that I have failed to explain how the concept of the "vestigial" relates to the "uncanny." That the uncanny in the form of the double, or doppelgänger in literature, is, as Freud notes in this footnoted anecdote, a remnant of infantile narcissism, a return of the repressed. This Freudian concept of the double a precursor to his notion of the death drive, that the child sees multiple versions of the self and feels calmed into immortality. Sofia also sends me new research on what is now considered the functions of the appendix. "Amazing to think that this weird 'useless' organ has evolved more than thirty times! It's haunting us," she writes to me.

as opposed to thinking merely about beauty, which feels more closed, some pretense at coherence.

There is something uncanny I think to walking around the space of this exhibit, the space shared by these two artists, mirroring or perhaps refracting each other in this proximity. In an interview, when thinking of the relationship between the viewer and her work, B. Ingrid Olson wishes for a "temporarily shared subjecthood." I share a space with them, thinking through their works. The viewer occupies their space, they occupy each other's. Their eyes become our eyes.[5]

While staring at these images on my computer screen, trying to imagine them in a physical space through virtual space, I flip through a chapter of a book by Elizabeth Grosz on insect spatiality and psychotic space. Did you know that some insects perform a mimesis that is actually grotesque and self-destructive? An insect camouflaged as a leaf can be cannibalized by another mistaking it for a leaf. The blurring and confusing of viewer with environment. The subject is unable to locate itself in space. Binaries collapse: inside and outside, mind and body, self and other.

When I look at the photographic compositions of B. Ingrid Olson, I think of how mirrors can trouble and dissemble. The artist photographs in a series of mirrors, posing with her own ceramic sculptures, masks, prostheses. The studio becomes a laboratory, a

5. When working on this talk, and when editing it afterwards, when attempting to write this footnote in fact, I soothe the baby by walking her past our mirrored closet, back and forth. I cannot tell yet whether she finds it soothing to see my face above hers, or whether to see her own, or some combination of the two.

site of experimentation. References haunt from Freud's essay: eyes, mirrors, dolls, doubles. The self as doll, doppelgänger in eerie lighting (Hans Bellmer's *poupées*, Bellmer tying up and photographing Unica Zürn, the private masochist performances of Ana Mendieta and Rudolf Schwarzkogler, the photographs as traces). Except, with Olson, the body is not limpid, it is taut. More intertextuality: when I look at the Olson image, the legs cut off, I see an echo of Joan Jonas's "Mirror Piece I," the body as uncanny vessel, Jonas repeating stories from Borges's *Labyrinths*. What are we looking at—four legs, two arms, what?

What am I looking at?: This is the strangeness of the work. The project, I think: to abstract the body, to other the self-portrait. "I do not make self-portraits," Olson says in an interview. The self becomes no longer coherent, no longer easily locatable in space. Can the viewer place this body part, where is it positioned, how is it cut off? This estrangement and intimacy (to be able to reach inside through the face of the plexiglas, into the hollow, and want to touch the image). To obscure, fragment, double. In the space of the gallery, another sort of labyrinth. Sculptures at crotch view, eye view.

There's a ghostliness, speaking someone else's image. I am reminded of Borges's 1945 essay "On Dubbing," one of his page-long pieces of film criticism. Someone else's voice comes out of another's image. In this doubling on the screen, the I is not I. Borges traces the phenomenon of dubbing back to the Holy Trinity, then to the chimera imagined by the Greeks. Something monstrous, he says, to this false mirror. Another voice implanted, another language—isn't that what I'm asked to do in this talk, to translate? And what is a talk, but a performance aware of the body in space, a dimensional text? Because I am drawn to the tangential lately, I linger on the singular footnote: "More than one spectator will ask himself: Since they are usurping voices, why not faces?"

Why not faces? A collage is a chimera, a strange combination. Faces disembodied, haunting. Like Olson, Klein's works are about perception and estrangement, transforming the familiar and famous image into something unable to be exactly deciphered. The representation of women in cinema and photo-novels, two double narratives playing soundless like a dream, the text from elsewhere, hidden, or buried. What am I looking at? Or: What am I reading? The departure for both artists from representing women, the self-portrait, the recognizable face, into something more abstract, and subtle.

In an interview, B. Ingrid Olson considers her photo compositions as a form of text, as a result of reading: "Something like an ellipsis, or a statement that almost turns into a question…when a footnote is used to expand on a facet of an idea, as a visibly separate explanation, a tangent alongside the primary text." As with Klein, these are readerly artworks, fragments of an infinite library.

It is the fragments at the edges that are the most interesting. The tape running through Astrid Klein's collaged images: like footnotes or tangents. Printed on the tape, tiny typewritten words that almost are imperceptible. Klein so aware that type has a face as well. I make connections: that the typewriter text from this show is from Arno Schmidt's *Zettel's Traum*, translated in English as *Bottom's Dream*, a massive text of 1334 pages considered almost impossible to translate because of its form—published originally as a photoset of typewritten pages composed in three columns, about the German translator of

Edgar Allen Poe. How Klein plays with scale, how tiny her footnotes, how large her wall collages. I wish often for writing to do what sculpture and collage does. How can writing achieve dimensionality, be aware of space? A paragraph like a frame, a box or a room. Can one walk around a paragraph?

All while thinking through this investigation into the uncanny that is an aesthetic investigation—what can double, return, echo—I keep on thinking of the phrase *mise en abyme*, a copy within a copy. André Gide in a journal passage wishes for literature to be like this, fiction within a fiction. Again how can literature yearn towards art, how can image ghost text? If I understand it right, this is what I'm doing here—performing a copy within a copy, a strange and uncertain essay about a strange or uncertain essay. In one of Borges's shorter nonfiction pieces, he conjures up Velazquez's "Las Meninas," the famous *mise en abyme*, the painting within a painting, with the reflection in the mirror at its center, while thinking back to an image on a biscuit tin from his childhood that replicated infinitely, its "vertiginous mystery." Something about this longing towards what he wants to write towards, "the problem of infinity." He quotes Schopenhauer, that dreaming and wakefulness can be experienced in reading the same pages of a single book—that in wakefulness one reads in a linear way, and in dreaming one skips around and flips, takes strange tangents, falls asleep, wakes up, returns. I am paraphrasing. I wish I had my silver shiny copy of *Labyrinths* in front of me, but I am finishing this appendix in a hurry on a plane to give this talk, as Leo sleeps, her little mouth open, snoring on her father. When we land, I should write Sofia and ask her if she knows the passage. Most likely she is reading it now.

Appendix D

THE PREPARATION OF THE BODY

HEAD

I would like to speak, at the beginning, of the *appendix*—that which is seen as unnecessary or excessive to the *body* of a text. I'm not sure of the exact etymology or origin of referring to the main text as a body—but that is how I think of it. Perhaps this is less from the history of the codex and more from staring at a Microsoft Word document, as I am now, preparing these notes—the outline of a body, the header and footnotes. I came up with this idea of writing these appendices, to my recently published book, *Book of Mutter*, out of a desire to gesture to the many variations of the project both future and past that are absent or missing from the final, printed version, which has a spine (more text as body) and an ISBN and blurbs, although I did not have the blurbs printed on the back of the book. This is now Appendix D, which I'm entitling at the head "The Preparation of the Body." On a recent letter of application to a full-time teaching job that I will most likely not get, at the college where I have adjuncted for five years, I defined the appendix project as writing on failure and the attempt at literature, written in the

Talk given at Washington University, October 19, 2017

shadow of *Book of Mutter*. Since the book has been out I have been asked to a handful of universities, such as this one, where I'm speaking today, to give an expected performance of the precariat and untenured mind. Because of this the appendices have been born as talks, rather than in the form of lists, notes, definitions, elaborations etc. I have not always been asked to deliver talks at these university events. Sometimes I am told, although I don't believe that was an option for tonight, that I could instead read from *Book of Mutter*. I think it's fair to say that I came up with the idea of writing these notes, or talks, out of a primary desire to *not* read from *Book of Mutter*, and instead to keep gesturing to its incompleteness and ongoingness, which connects, for me, to the fragmentary project of literature, and what I long for in writing. It is not lost on me the paradox or at least the ambivalence at work here—I have refused to read from the published text, and yet I'm also, in these appendix talks, refusing to let go of it, which I think is a form of what publication is supposed to be—a letting go of the text for the writer, giving it over to the reader, with, usually, some expected public mediation on the part of the author. My desire not to read from the published book, but rather to consider instead what I took out over more than a decade—its many ruptures and failings, variations and iterations—is a desire that parallels Roland Barthes's various writing projects that came out of his grief through the loss of his mother. In what would become the last two years of his life, Barthes's writing projects sought to resist somehow the book as a Monument. Yet this is also a dialectical desire, because elsewhere Barthes wishes for his unwritten book on his mother to stand as a Monument—the conflicting desires of the writer, to be both private and public, which is also the conflicting desires of grief.

In his introductory lecture, given on December 2, 1978, for what would become his last lecture series at the Collège de France, on *The Preparation of the Novel*, Barthes gestures to this ongoing project, these talks he has been giving for several years. He notes that he decided, after some thought, not to publish his lectures on *The Neutral*, noting that "I think that part of life's activity should always be set aside for the *Ephemeral*. What happens only once and vanishes, it's the necessary share of the rejected Monument, and therein lies the vocation of the Course…" A talk or lecture, he notes, is a specific production, a mix of writing and oration. A lecture is in the moment. It cannot be repeated. It can be recorded, or published, or archived, but a lecture or talk really exists in an intimate and present, or hopefully present, public, and cannot be experienced by everyone. People have suggested I should just repeat these talks. After all, they take weeks of time to think through and write, sometimes a month, but it's not the project. The project has nothing to do with repeating the talk, or rereading them, and hopefully I can resist publishing them in any concrete way. Not wanting the appendix project published, at least as a book, is out of a desire, not only to reject the Monument, but also a desire to not have to talk in public about another book, to avoid going through the requisite author activities, but here again is another paradox—for here I am, talking about the appendix project. It feels like a necessary act, at this point where I am as a writer, and also as a published author, to re-engage in a passionate way in the ephemeral and daily practice of the writer, a way of returning back to the semi-privacy of writing—the different forms this might take—the letter, the notebook, and the talk. A talk however, Barthes notes, is not quite a performance. A talk is an outline for writing and speaking, a means to prepare and vocalize one's thoughts. This is a talk, in that in order for it to truly exist I must read the words out loud to at least a handful of people. The talk is a different mode of writing than the body of a book. In a piece of writing, the author's body is absent, but in a talk I must by its very nature be present in the room. But this appendix talk is in many ways an essay, in that I wrote it all down. There is little room for improvisation. Barthes meticulously typed up his notes for his lectures, which read like one long unfolding monologue, and then he recollected them in manuscript afterwards. Because of his untimely death, this manuscript is the last manuscript of Barthes that we have. I too type up these talks, and think of them as writing, but different, somehow, from other forms of writing. It's really a draft, although delivered live. Overall, I have been dissatisfied with them, although people seem to like them. Because my talks are usually supposed to be from 40–50 minutes, they have read as too long, in long unbroken paragraphs. They usually range from 5000–6000 words. Because I feel pressured to say something specific, or useful, about writing or literature, I fear they bear too much the brunt of a thesis statement. I like that they wear some-how the time of their creation. This is something that the talk can do, like Borges writing seven lectures over seven nights towards the end of his life. Maybe because he was blind, Borges's later essays also have the feeling of a recorded talk. He speaks in his lecture on blindness that he's noticed, after all these years of giving talks, that people tend to like the concrete, specific, and personal, as opposed to the more abstract. I began the appendix project when my daughter was a newborn. She was three months old when I gave my first talk, at the Printed Matter bookstore in New York, and it was the first time my partner and I had been out of the apartment without her. It seems whenever I have to write an appendix Leo goes through a sleep regression, as she is now, at over ten months old, as I get ready to leave with her and John for St. Louis tomorrow morning (the strange performance of the talk—drafted in the days before the time it is delivered). We are up every morning at 4am, and we begin the day then, grinding coffee, taking out the dog, letting Leo play with her books and blocks. At the same time, she is refusing to go to bed until much later, and then wakes up several times in the night. The effect is something like one ongoing day without end. So many of Leo's books are about distinguishing the day and the night, but these divisions are not clear to me anymore, especially lately. It seems I always complain in these talks of not sleeping. I seem to only be able to work on the appendix project when I am too tired to do anything else. Or, it seems when I am too tired to do anything else, I can only work on the appendix project. There's a porousness and slowness that comes with exhaustion, I think, where I can see through the different iterations and variations of a work's potential, where I can somehow relive grief, both the grief of composing this book, and the grief of losing my mother. A sort of aphasic openness, where I approach these ideas absent of certain language, knowing almost nothing. The deep fatigue becomes a filter, like a gauze or glaze.

HOLDS AND HOUSES

I read in a recent interview with Anne Carson that when she sets out to write an essay, which often take the shape of talks or lectures, she has about six books in front of her, and the task of writing is to write about how they connect with each other. For this appendix I have in front of me a book on Walter Benjamin and the archive, W. G.

Sebald's *Austerlitz*, Bhanu Kapil's *Ban en Banlieue* and *Schizophrene*, Theresa Hak Kyung Cha's *Dictee*, Roland Barthes's *The Preparation of the Novel*, and somewhat permanently on the top of the couch, Anne Carson's *Nox*, which my baby this morning keeps on taking out and playing with, opening the box, pulling at the accordion pages. On my desk somewhere I have a copy of *Book of Mutter*, that I pulled out from a box in the closet, which is underneath a garbage bag of outgrown baby clothes, but I don't open it. What I want to think about is not there.

I want to meditate upon a feeling after a book is published that is a longing, that the work is not finished, the project still ongoing. And how can works, like the ones I just mentioned, house this spirit, of the unfinished or ongoing, which is the notes. My friend, the writer Sofia Samatar, often speaks of a desire for a book to have *a feeling of the posthumous*, or, she sometimes clarifies, in our many email exchanges, *a feeling of the notebook*. We often speak about this feeling, or longing, in opposition to the feeling of preparing a book for publication, which involves editing out everything unclear or confusing to a reader, the work taking another sort of shape, the confining one of a published book. Writing of the project of these talks, Sofia writes somewhat in envy that a talk doesn't have to undergo as much the task of being shaped for publication. There can be more freedom of movement. A talk can feel more like a draft of thought, an outline of a body.

Beginning with the head of the book and moving down, I want to meditate upon a quote from Walter Benjamin, from "The Writer's Technique in Thirteen Theses" in his *One-Way Street*: "The work is the death mask of its conception." Once a work begins, there is the assumption that it must end. That it cannot exist in process, in notes. The work's life determines its death—a new life, for the reader. Benjamin called *One-Way Street* a notebook. It was his only book published in his lifetime beyond his dissertation, and it took the form of a fragmented collection of notes and aphorism. His writing process involved an elaborate archiving and notebooking system. These notebooks navigate across lines of research and thinking. The extreme economy of his handwriting echoing Robert Walser's microscripts handwritten on notebooks and scraps. Benjamin kept a notebook that was a table of contents of his other works, a sort of notebook of notebooks.

His various archival containers:

Folders
Files
Envelopes
Cases
Boxes

I like thinking about what forms contain writing. A book is a type of container. So is a box. How a work can feel like a container—like a box—what it holds and houses. Anne Carson's *Nox* is a box holding photocopied scraps, repetitions, photographs, diary entries, etymologies. Like an archive or artifact lost and then found. Asking how to write an elegy to a sibling who's disappeared? Posthumous feeling—a work that doesn't feel finished or contained. Posthumous feeling—the assumption that one doesn't have to finish or publish, or think of a published work for a reader or editor or publisher. The work can remain, raw and private and shiny.

I want to turn now to two scenes of burial in the books I am considering here. First, in W. G. Sebald's *Austerlitz*, the architecture historian Jacques Austerlitz, whose memories of being sent to Wales as a child refugee from Czechoslovakia have been buried, experiences a crisis of writing, a paralysis due to the dislocation of language. Sebald's *Austerlitz* is somewhat modeled on two itinerant travelers and thinkers: on Ludwig Wittgenstein, his notebooks carried around in a rucksack, and also on Benjamin, with his historical project on the Paris arcades, his proliferation of notes, quotations, sketches and photographs. As in Sebald's other works, the discovery of photographs or an album of photographs is essential to the narrative. There are many containers within Sebald's *Austerlitz*. Besides the various photo albums, and the rucksack containing notebooks, there is also an aviary and the cabinets of curiosities in the ancestral home of a schoolboy friend. At one point Austerlitz tells the narrator that he thought of collecting his fragmentary studies in a book. He made lists of their possible focus, from several volumes to a series of essays on a vast catalogue of potential topics, dealing with space and the city, but realized all he had was a mass of papers, of misdirected sketches. He became so paralyzed by the possibilities of language, and an aversion to his project, to these masses of bundles of paper, that he decided that he must somehow get rid of his vast archives, this weight he has been carrying around with him. Sebald writes, "One evening, said Austerlitz, I gathered up all my papers, bundled or loose, my notepads and exercise books, my files and lecture notes, anything with my writing on it, and carried the entire collection out of the house to the far end of the garden, where I threw it on the compost heap and buried it under layers of rotted leaves and spadefuls of earth." The gesture of throwing notes into the garden also begins Bhanu Kapil's *Schizophrene*, her work on mental illness and migration, of the post-Partition diaspora. In the opening text that functions like a prologue, she writes, "On the *night* I knew my book *had failed*, I threw it—in the form of a *notebook*, a handwritten final *draft*—into the garden of my *house* in Colorado Christmas Eve, 2007. It snowed that winter and into the spring; before the weather turned truly *warm*, I retrieved my *notes*, and began to write again, from the fragments, the phrases and lines still legible on the warped, decayed, but curiously rigid pages." In both of these passages, the compost heap or garden soil becomes the container housing the manuscripts in notes. Something fecund, the draft becomes part of the earth. She writes again from the notes. A longing for an impossible (posthumous?) form. A book that has been buried in the ground.

I would like to gesture to another way these two novels connect—that they both are about dislocation of place and language. These two texts of migration and aphasia. And the authors too—W. G. Sebald an itinerant German writing from England, Bhanu Kapil a British Punjabi writing from Colorado, and wondering through her recent works what it would be like to have written her books in England or in India. And that these narratives of violence and madness are impossible, are housed in silence, necessarily buried. How can one recover what is impossible (a childhood or home that has been removed and dislocated, a language, an identity)? What kind of book can contain the enforced silence of the home, of family, the unwriting of violence and separation?

In the first lecture, Barthes writes about his fantasy for a novel—*Vita Nova*, after Dante, a novel about the death of his mother. He references the date of April 15, 1978, this moment of *satori* or enlightenment while traveling, where he experiences what he calls a "literary conversion." It is on this date that he suddenly realizes a desire for a new writing life and considers quitting his teaching position in order to write. He realizes he needs to shake himself out of the monotony of his grief. He describes bereavement as a fold (I think of the accordion fold binding of Anne Carson's *Nox*, her numb and fragmented elegy to the death of her prodigal brother). Before/After. This I understand—how grief can be transformative, can catalyze a new writing process, the desire for new forms. For now he will devote himself to considering the fantasy of this novel, *Vita Nova*, in a series of lectures. *The Preparation of a Novel* begins not with writing, but with a longing, what he calls *Vouloir-Écrire*, which has been translated in two different ways, with different connotations: both "the will to write" or "the want to write." A "will to write" suggests something of a steely determination, or even discipline, or process. A "want to write" is nothing but longing. He is not, Barthes notes, actually writing a novel, but fantasizing about writing a novel. Barthes's lecture series prepares for the novel, but does not write it. The preparation of the novel, he writes, differs from the *fact* of writing. One of the questions Barthes thinks through is how to work the fragmented notes of the present and of the day into a new form. One of the main ways one prepares for a novel, Barthes theorizes, is by taking notes, a practice he calls *notatio*. For this practice of writing in a notebook, one needs time. In a wonderful equation, he considers the notebook as the object which houses notes that think through a novel. This equation is a little difficult to read out loud, and shows the abbreviated form of some of his lecture notes from which he then digressed, but I'll attempt it:

"the notebook, not very thick -> pockets? Modern clothing, no one wears jackets anymore ≠ Flaubert's notebooks, in beautiful black moleskin; Proust's Summer: fewer notes!"

Barthes is imagining not only the writing style but also the notebook style of these writers he loves so dearly—Flaubert's moleskine, Kafka's octavos—the writer slipped these notebooks into his jacket, he imagines, what a 19th century premise, how to be a novelist now, in this modern age, how did Proust take notes in the summer! It's important to think too that Barthes was preparing a seminar on photographs of Proust's social circle—no doubt he spent time staring with delight at these three-piece suits and houndstooth trousers. A failure of the imagination to Barthes's lectures, this writer I love and think to more than anyone else lately and want to emulate in turn—that he only envisions the novelist taking notes as the romantic mode of male bachelor dandy.

APPENDIX

In a letter, Benjamin characterizes his *Arcades Project* as the "theater of all my struggles and ideas." I like thinking of a writing project as a sort of theater, and what encapsulates the project is not just the final book, but also its many performances, practices, and stagings. Bhanu Kapil's *Ban en Banlieue* reads like a theater of struggles and ideas, the longing for a novel and its many incarnations that only appear in fragments in the text, circling around the character of Ban, a brown (black) girl living in the suburbs of London, walking home from the 1979 race riots. All while tracing through notes on performance, blog entries, notebooks, drafts, and various errata, other bodies deemed as disposable or silenced, the most notable haunting being Nirbhaya, "The Fearless One," the young woman gang-raped and beaten to death on a bus in New Delhi in 2012. This work, that comes after *Schizophrene*, reads much like Benjamin's elaborate archiving system, the preparations for putting together a book, and simultaneously, the energy against it, a sort of refusal. It begins with an outline of a body of a text, a subversion of a table of contents, including preface, end-notes, epigraphs, blurbs, and appendix. In her Butcher's Block Appendix to *Ban en Banlieue*, she notes that 97.5% of the work of *Ban* happened in both private and public notebooks (her public notebook in the form of a blog). She creates a physical stack of these notes, printing out the pages of her blog, and stacking her actual notebooks onto a neighbor's discarded butcher's block slab. She composes the appendix through a gesture of bibliomancy, she picks a single quote at random from each of these notebooks to include in the then published appendix. Throughout Kapil plays with the multiplicity of a novel, all of its potential iterations. Her book was a failure, but not an interesting one, Kapil writes in *Ban en Banlieue*, of the different variations and drafts of this project throughout the years. Of course, I don't think this is true. And yet, so much of the energy of the book is circling around this failure—the impossibility and refusal to write a coherent narrative of the narrator's childhood, the refusal to be a good post-colonial subject. And if a book is not a failure, would we continue to write towards it?

When writing this section on the appendix, I'm remembering how my mother's appendix had to be removed a year before she died. Later, we were told that this was a sign of impending death—the failure of the appendix—the need for this organ to be removed. The suddenness of the surgery. The ambulance in the night.

DOUBT IS DOUBLE

At the opening of *Ban en Banlieue*, Bhanu Kapil takes Theresa Hak Kyung Cha's *Dictee* off the shelf and opens to a page at random. Another performance of bibliomancy. Both *Ban* and *Dictee* have the feeling of the manuscript, or the posthumous. People often think that *Dictee* was published posthumously. But Theresa Hak Kyung Cha died a week after *Dictee* was published, murdered in New York City at the age of 31. Still, the book, which she prepared for publication, has a posthumous feel. I believe this is because the book has the quality of an archive. There is a quality of the ephemeral to *Dictee*, something like a box or album (the anatomical illustrations, the map of a divided Korea). The *Thalia* section of *Dictee*. The section that refuses narrative. A handwritten letter and a typewritten letter to a mysterious Mrs. Claxton. Which reminds me of an earlier thread in *Book of Mutter*, where I included the redacted FBI Files of Marilyn Monroe. I am now reading from a Word document marked September 6, 2010. I include various letters from a Ms. Alta Melton to J. Edgar Hoover, wondering whether Marilyn Monroe's death was a suicide or a murder. A section I later removed. In *Ban en Banlieue*, Kapil reveals the feeling of a book in process, or the ghosts of its past iterations. Kapil performs and records the process of composing on screen—press click, press delete, move to another file. A desire to document the ephemeral, she includes a list of her talks and performances she's given circling around *Ban*. Her own preparation of the novel. Failed sections. Deleted epigraphs.

I wish I had preserved more the failures, the sense of drafts. How *Book of Mutter* once existed entirely as notes, attempts, drafts, folders, and those iterations still exist, but they are not in the final book. I wish somehow I could have shown the cyclical nature in which I worked on it. The awful rejections and edits. My own suffering with this project.

A deleted section:

> Of Septimus Smith, the Woolfman, writing down conspiracy theories on scraps of paper.

> "It would shape itself something like that but now, at this moment, sitting stuck there with an empty seat beside him, nothing shaped itself at all. It was all in scraps and fragments."

A deleted epigraph from an early version of the mother book, taken from Thomas Bernhard's *Extinction* (his last novel?):

> It's not enough to make notes about something that's important to us, perhaps more important than anything else, I said, namely the whole complex of our origins. It's not enough to have filled so many hundreds and thousands of strips of paper on the subject, a subject that encompasses our whole life. We must produce a substantial account, not to say a long account,

of what we emerged from, what we are made of and what has *determined our being* for as long as we've lived.

That this was printed out on a strip of paper and taped above my desk for as long as I remember, like a manifesto of sorts.

I want to write to that facsimile of the crossed-out manuscript in *Dictee*, that spread of pages. I think my desire for *Book of Mutter* to have felt more like a manuscript is a desire for it to feel more in preparation, in process. A desire for doubt. Doubt comes from the root "duo" or "two." A manuscript contains doubt, it doubles back on itself. It's a space where you amend and obliterate what's written. Where you cross out. What was and what is no longer.

The brackets in *Ban en Banlieue*. Suggested other words, like a manuscript in process. A desire for, a longing for a sentence that's a form of incubation. In *Preparation of the Novel* Barthes rhapsodizes on the metaphysics of Flaubert's sentences. I need to open a dossier on the sentence, he writes. A dossier for Barthes is a hypothetical and ongoing file of thought that will produce something else, a topic for another lecture, more notes. He is thinking through the sentence in connection with thinking through the haiku. Short forms, he thinks, is what one starts with, to prepare for a novel.

"Brackets are exciting," Anne Carson writes in the foreword to her translation of Sappho. In her brackets, not every gap or illegibility is indicated. They are an "aesthetic gesture toward the papryological event rather than an accurate read of it." An epigraph from Sappho begins *Dictee*. The fragments that are buried and then unearthed. What is legible; what is guessed at; what remains lost entirely.

I'm going over what's been removed, the bracketed, that only I can see. That's what Anne Carson is doing with Sappho—attempting to recover what is not there. To guess at what may have been next to the text that we do have, but which remains unknown. How to preserve what's crossed out?

The original handwritten draft of Sebald's *Austerlitz* had the character Austerlitz burn the manuscript instead of burying it in the compost heap, echoing Nabokov burning the first chapter of Lolita. (Kafka asking Max Brod to burn his manuscripts.) To destroy previous drafts. A refusal of the monument or the archive? (Bhanu Kapil— "No, I don't think so. I press delete.")

Narrative's urges—towards a novel, towards stories—and then, in *Ban en Banlieue*, this beautiful, ravaging impossibility. What can writing do? What can the book do? What can performance do, the body defiant in public, in protest, in demonstration, a body silent and refusing in an institutional setting, at a talk or panel, that literature fails at? And how can that disappearance and documentation be then traced in a book? How can a book contain somehow the furious energy of its failure, of its processes, its drafts, its many notebooks?

FOLDER

After two years of lectures on *Preparation of a Novel*, all Barthes produced of *Vita Nova* is an eight page handwritten outline, now published as an appendix. I want to now meditate upon the facsimile of the eight page outline housed in a cardboard red folder. The first seven pages handwritten in ink on blank typewriter paper, the last on grid paper. Only notes, sketching out something of a loose outline. On almost every page at the top "Prologue." At the bottom: "Epilogue."

I began with eight pages of notes in which to attempt to write this talk, and at the end, I have the eight pages of Barthes's outline, of a book about the body of his dead mother. An outline—the body as a fragmentary and unwritten text. From head to appendix to epilogue. What escapes outside of the book? How to contain these feelings? Where does the thinking now go?

How time worked at the end, almost exactly a year ago. The contractions began on Halloween, which is when we found out she was dying those years before. How I would labor at night, and be up in the day. And then for a month of contractions, false contractions, how every date began to take on a strange and ghostly meaning, where I was reliving also my childhood, her illness, sometimes at the same time. I would forget she was dead. I felt I was talking to her.

I labored for 24 hours and gave birth in the morning
My mother's two days—that was a labor too
The body has to prepare to die and prepare to give birth.

But when I was pregnant, she was so close to me. I was so close to my childhood. Like some door was open. The month of prodromal labor, contractions in the night. Those two weeks of lumbering around, two weeks overdue, my daughter refusing to come out of me. How sore and exhausted I felt. And somehow childlike. The refusal. Trump. I will not bring a daughter into this world. On the table at the Chinese medicine doctor in the Upper West Side to be given a series of electric acupuncture needles in my lower back and ass, in order to attempt to induce labor. The excruciating reflexology massage then part of the procedure. I had to try to relax and have faith that she wouldn't actually break the bones in my hand, my feet, my shoulders, pushing the baby down, down. I had the procedure done over two days, with Thanksgiving in between. The baby dropped but not enough. On the first day a contraction came and I had an out of body experience—I was naked, on the table, alone in the room, listening to "Für Elise" through the walls, playing on a tiny radio in the next room. The door was open, and people would walk by and see me naked and silently contorting on the table, my naked ass sticking out. How in that stage of pregnancy all privacy retreats, so much like dying. The door was open. I could see into my past. I am a child playing "Für Elise" on the piano in the front room, the room that was reserved for Christmas and formal occasions. The orange shag rug, the matching orange chairs. How '70s. My mother was there. I needed her there. I felt certain that I was going to die, or that I had already died.

Earlier that morning I was at my midwives' office, getting another cervical sweep, which was also excruciating, I screamed and begged my midwife to take her finger out of me, to stop. We went slowly. I tried counting to 20 each time. The practice shared an office with several other doctors in the cramped space, including a psychiatrist who specialized in patients with dementia. That day an elderly woman was in the waiting room, flanked by her two aides, screaming at the top of her lungs. She was suffering. I closed my eyes and focused on her voice, instead of the pain of the cervical sweep, which somehow made it more bearable, the absurdity of this. And suddenly—a flash—I was at the hospital, in the cafeteria, my mother on the ward with the senile patients, why had they put her there?

Sitting with my mother, my mother aphastic, broken, herself aged by the medicines, the suffering, aged and yellowed, and listening to all the screams around me. Like a flash. I was back there. I had refused to think about that time at all.

But I couldn't and shouldn't add this to the book. Because I have already written it. It is at the printers…I thought coming back to on the table.

And perhaps this was my satori, my moment of awakening. That the book was not finished, it was ongoing. That there are many versions until there is the final version. And even then there are many versions. The container wasn't a book but my body. That my body is a space where the text was still being written. That my body is the archive.

Appendix E

THE ART OF DISEUSE

THAT WHICH IS VESTIGIAL

Over the years of reading Theresa Hak Kyung Cha's *Dictee*, I keep on misreading the title of the second fragmented text that begins the book, a prose poem entitled DISEUSE. Until recently, I read the title as DISEASE, and then other times as DIS-USE, as in not in use, as opposed to DISEUSE, which is a French term for a female monologist, a concept I will get to later on in this talk. The short fragmented opening text is a performance of stutter, of a second language, the physicality and punctuation of the speaker and spoken.

> She mimicks the speaking. That might resemble speech. (Anything at all.) Bared noise, groan, bits torn from words. Since she hesitates to measure the accuracy, she resorts to mimicking gestures with her mouth.

Language is experienced here as an occupation and violation, by an immigrant speaker who has language imposed on her, who must learn to repeat, an expected echo, in English and French.

Talk given at Poetry Project, October 27, 2017

The breakdown of the body forcing itself to rework its relationship to the sound of new words. The pain of mimicry. The language here is of deformation and excess, a swollenness. Also, the process is of hollowing out, of removing the tumors (as if to impose a language is to impose a disease).

> She allows others. In place of her. Admits others to make full. Make swarm. All barren cavities to make swollen. The others each occupying her. Tumorous layers, expel all excesses until in all cavities she is flesh.

DIS-USE also makes a sort of sense as the title of Cha's section, and for me to begin this talk, which is another appendix. What is an appendix but what's disused, or no longer in use. Like how language can be vestigial—in the case of Cha's *Dictee*—the Korean language as a mother tongue which must be hidden or abandoned. Which cannot be used. Or the French—which is excessive, extra.

During *dictee*, or dictation, you write down what the teacher is saying. The opening page of Cha's text parodies such a language exercise. Here the *dictee* is made literal, including the punctuation, making unfamiliar and slightly wrong the act of dictation, these spaces between two languages:

> Open paragraph   It was the first day   period
> She had come from a far   period

Although I've thought about Cha's *Dictee*, her text of mothers and mother tongues, for perhaps a decade, almost as long as I attempted my book on my mother, and although it influenced the text and thinking about the book in a way that feels like a ghost or hallucination, I've written little about it. Even when thinking about the book again this past month or so, I've managed to write down very little about what others have referred to as a decolonizing text. As I've rearranged these words on the page, in order to make a talk, in order to talk—I feel myself stuttering. Who gets to speak for a dead woman's text? In *Dictee*, who speaks for someone else to write it down? Is it Cha's mother, and her daughter is the writer-narrator? Is it all of the martyr-mothers and revolutionaries who crowd the text, Joan of Arc, Yu Guan Soon, and Cha writes them down, she is the teller? Is it all of the many scholars of Cha, whose theoretical language and analysis I pilfer and borrow from, rearrange, introduce with errors? Is Cha the *Diseuse* as well as the *Dictee*?

Last month my baby daughter was ill with a bad cold, a week with many sounds (coughing, crying, soothing, that chortling suction of sucking out snot with a tube) but without much language. Throughout that feverish week, I kept on seeing Cha's book lying on top of my daughter's board book of *Madeline* over on the bedside table, a juxtaposition that in my sleep-deprived state, much like my misreading, I began to make something out of. The parallel felt clear, although somewhat off and wrong, porous and unsure, as connections can feel when one hasn't had sleep. What a rigid and moralizing text *Madeline* is, such strange cozy conformity. I can now memorize and recite almost the entire book. "In two straight lines they broke their bread, brushed their teeth and went to bed." And of course, little Madeline, the tiny American at the strict boarding school or convent in Paris often scolded for leaving those two little lines. Who has to—of course, of course!—have her appendix removed.

My daughter at 11 months today is learning to speak. We teach her how. She points at our dog and says dog. She points at a picture of a dog and says dog. Yes, that's right, we say to her. Dog. Dog dog dog dog dog. She had an illness for a week, an ear infection, and came out of it babbling new words. At first she just speaks new sounds, a peal or string of them, then over time we help teach her how to shape them into recognizable objects that are words. Yes, that's dog. Yes, that's cat. Yes, that's dada. Yes, that's mama.

At the Convent of the Sacred Heart in San Francisco, which Cha began to attend as a teenager, once she moved to the States with her family, she studied ancient Greek and Latin, sang in the chorus, and learned to speak and write in English and French. There is something of the convent atmosphere to *Dictee*, as if it were here that this book began to take up space within her body. In one of the opening sections, Cha plays with the expected mimicry of the Ash Wednesday mass. In this section Cha tells us that *dictee* is every Friday, for an hour before Mass, like a prayer. The rigidness and repetitiveness of the catechism, in its choreography and recitations. The Novena—repeat nine times.

> First Friday. One hour before mass. Mass every First Friday. Dictée first. Every Friday. Before mass. Dictée before. Back in the study hall. It is time. Snaps once. One step right from the desk. Single file. Snaps twice. Follow single line.

My early encounters with language were that of rigidity. The repetition and memorization of words, phrases, state capitols, songs. Repeat after me. I remember how in Catholic school we would have to make straight lines on sheets of paper with a ruler, and then practice our handwriting, over and over, our writing must move in between these two straight lines, like good little girls, just like Madeline. I remember the way the pencil would leave a red and sore impression on my finger. How I would never be able to draw these lines straight. How much I practiced, to make my handwriting so neat. Why were Catholic schools so obsessed with handwriting?

Sofia is taking German now, and she writes me of all the scribbled exercises in the workbooks you do when learning the language, and yet they don't say anything. They hold time, they're durational, you do them every day, at regular hours, she writes. And they're full of errors. I remember, with Sofia writing me this, all of the German language exercises that were originally in *Book of Mutter*, all of the bracketed instructions dealing with language, etymologies, translations, definitions, that were no doubt inspired by the parody of language textbooks that begins *Dictee*. When I began the book I was taking a community German class at the Goethe Institut in downtown Chicago, with a tyrant of a German teacher. His mode of instruction was to humiliate us until we pronounced a word correctly. There was something that called back to me the atmosphere of Catholic school, that presentation and expectation, but the dread and anxiety of not knowing language, of not being good enough. How Cha performs the physicality and interiority of such dread and anxiety. How the acquisition of language can be about power and mastery and control.

When I read *Dictee*, the question I think the most about is how to read a text of such privacy and opacity. I now realize so much that I removed from *Book of Mutter*, in terms of the structures of language, was to make the text easily translatable. That I desired opacity in a text, but I bowed to pressures for lucidity or clarity. I like, as others have written, how the text asks the question: how can readers approach the book if they are not fluent in English, French, Korean, Chinese, Ancient Greek and Latin? The book resists mastery. Every time I read it, it is like a secret I attempt to decipher. This is most apparent in the opening frontispiece of the book, the verso of the title page, that is easily skipped over. It is an image of scratches of language in white on a black background. In its translation from the Korean, the passage reads:

Mother
I Miss You
I'm Hungry
I want to Go Home

The image is of a wall in what appears to be either a cave or a mine. It is thought to be an inscription carved into a tunnel by Korean laborers in Japan, meant to provide an escape for the Japanese emperor during WWII. And yet, the provenance and origins of this inscription is still debated, whether this was written during the war or afterwards, and by whom. The language is of protest, exile, and longing, in a context of colonial oppression, but the translations and possible readings are multiple and porous, vague and sketchy, which Cha plays up with her bad photocopy of the image. The vestigial nature of Korean in Cha's text, its trace remains, as a ghost language. In the devastating section "Calliope/Epic Poetry," Cha writes of her mother, Huo Hyung Soon, who can only speak Korean in private as she was born in exile in Manchuria, where her family moved to escape the Japanese occupation. "You are Bilingual," Cha writes. "You are Tri-lingual. The tongue that is forbidden is your own mother tongue."

AN ARTIST IN TALKING—an intermission

Diseuse is the feminine of the French for *diseur* or "teller," a derivative of *dire*, to tell. The *diseuse* is the art of the female monologue. The art of talking, but in the voice or voices of women. What makes this monologue particularly female or feminine, I wonder. Something divine about the elasticity of such talk, perhaps, like the Cumaen Sibyl at Delphi. A teller suggests something like this. The term enters English usage in the context of the theater from the last decade of the 19th century, most likely imported when the French cabaret singer Yvette Guibert toured New York City in the mid-1890s. The bawdy patter of her songs. The most famous American known for the art of the diseuse was probably Ruth Draper, whose speaking portraits crowded the stage with imaginary figures. She had such a facility for languages—English, French, German, Italian, and her characters also featured accents that were made-up versions of other languages, like her indeterminate Slavic accent. I am told on Ruth Draper's Wikipedia that her monologues were known to induce "real hallucination" in audience members. I listen to fragments of audio on a website dedicated to her. Perhaps the audience couldn't believe she was speaking all of these voices herself.

HER OWN PRIVATE THEATER

This is a talk about talkers. When I think of the *diseuse*, and merge it with disease, I think of Anna O., the pseudonym of Bertha Pappenheim, Josef Breuer's young Viennese *fräulein* who became the first psychoanalytic case study of hysteria. The case study of

Anna O. is the tale of a daughter/diseuse, but another writes down the words of the speaker, in this case Dr. Breuer. Even though Anna O. was Breuer's patient, Sigmund Freud (but not Anna O. herself) is also viewed as the co-author of the case study of the female talker Anna O. Reading the case study of Anna O. is like reading through an opaque glass, the voice in the jar that is the Cumaen Sibyl. I am interested in how a text can contain sound. The text reads like a report of a series of monologues in many voices and languages. I realize, looking at my heavily underlined copy of my *Freud Reader*, which I've had since grad school, how important the Anna O. case study was in the development of my book about my mother, which is a book about language and madness, when the rhythm of muttering was more of the attempted cadence of the book. When I imagined the sounds and voices of the text bouncing off the pages, like walls.

We are told at the beginning of the case study that Anna O. possessed "great poetic and imaginative gifts," and that while she did her daughterly duties in her strict household, her housework and hosting, she would often immerse herself in daydreaming, what Breuer calls "her own private theater." After nursing her sick father nonstop, she collapsed from nervous exhaustion. This catalyzed an onset of an illness beginning with a severe cough, and various paralyses, then descending into what Breuer diagnoses as paraphasia, or disturbances of speech. We are told that during this illness she alternated through different states of consciousness at different times during the day. In the afternoon, she entered a somnolent state, what Breuer calls "absences," putting the word itself in quotations, where she forgets who she is. It is during the afternoon that her *conditione second* emerges, her hallucinations, what Breuer terms her "naughtiness," which included saying things and throwing things, like cushions. At some point, we are told, her condition deteriorates, and during a period of four months she takes to bed and remains. She continues a period of waking at night, and sleeping in the afternoons, the same nocturnal rhythm as when she exhaustively nursed her father.

What is most remarkable about Anna O.'s hysteria is her disintegrating and sometimes poetic relationship to language. I want to speak about how profound and weird Anna O.'s relationship is to her native language, which is German, and to language in general. I like to imagine that Theresa Hak Kyung Cha was reading or had read Anna O. when composing her own *Dictee*. Although, I'm not sure it matters. There is something here, about what happens when one loses language. Cha's mother is forbidden from speaking Korean and must speak it only in secret circles. This reminds me how in Sebald's *Austerlitz*, Jacques Austerlitz doesn't remember that his first language was Czech, so clouded over were his experiences before being put on the *kindertransport* to Wales, to escape the internment camps, and his memories of his childhood only begin to appear when he realizes he knows this other, now foreign language. Anna O. loses her German, sometimes completely. This happens at the same time as her paraphasia, or speech disturbances. Her speech became disorganized, degraded, and confused, and eventually for a period of time she loses her language entirely. For two weeks she is completely dumb. This is Breuer:

> It first became noticeable that she was at a loss to find words, and this difficulty gradually increased. Later she lost her command of grammar and syntax; she no longer conjugated

verbs, and eventually she used only infinitives, for the most part incorrectly formed from weak past participles; and she omitted both the definite and indefinite article. In the process of time she became almost completely deprived of words. She put them together laboriously out of four or five languages and became almost unintelligible.

Eventually, Breuer writes, he gets her to talk about what's bothering her, even though she does not wish to speak about it. And the extreme paraphasia recedes, he writes, but afterwards she only spoke in English. Sometimes she would also talk in French and Italian. She would understand German, but not speak it or write it. Eventually, after her father dies, she stopped being able to understand German entirely, preferring English, although she was able to read French and Italian, and even translate these languages into English. We are told she began writing again, but only Roman printed letters, copying the alphabet from her edition of Shakespeare. Earlier, before she began speaking exclusively English, it was noticed that during her episodes she was working out some sort of story or situation, as indicated by a few muttered phrases. When she comes to from her hallucinations she repeats the phrase over and over, "tormenting tormenting." If during her repeated complaints of "tormenting, tormenting," one of these other phrases was repeated, she would begin telling a story, first "hesitatingly and in her paraphrastic jargon," as Breuer writes, and then, over time, as her narrative became more coherent, in quite correct German, he writes. These fairytale-like stories often began with an anxious girl at a sickbed. After her father's death, he writes, the stories, often compelled during an evening hypnosis, became more tragic, and eventually became more nightmarish and hallucinatory, losing their coherence. Eventually, he writes, her proper German language returned to her when they were able to recreate the scene of the originary hallucination she had at her father's sickbed, actually moving the furniture so as to resemble her father's sickroom, and then recounting the hallucination in language.

There is something of Anna O.'s sickbed monologues that remind me of the legend of Virginia Woolf's aural hallucinations of birds singing a Greek chorus. Woolf recalls in "Old Bloomsbury," that when she was once sick in bed she imagined not only birds singing in Greek but also King Edward using foul language among the azaleas. The same year she published *Mrs. Dalloway*, Woolf published an essay, "On Not Knowing Greek," which was not about not knowing Greek, but about longing for and studying Greek grammar and the tragedies, which is in many ways about the desire to have had the education of any boy in her social class. Mrs Dalloway, too, wants to spend a decade just learning Greek.

Woolf gave these hallucinations of Greek-talking birds to her mad character Septimus Smith in *Mrs. Dalloway*. She was terrified that her writing would be thought incoherent. That no one would understand her meandering streams. That they would think she was Septimus Smith muttering unclear epiphanies on his little scraps of paper. So she ordered herself, she wrote wonderfully controlled passages, she ordered the chaos the confusion but there was that threat always that threat of the deep end that hint of hysteria

The voices oh the voices
The birds, the birds are singing their Greek chorus

Recently I read a review in the *London Review of Books* of Chris Kraus's biography of Kathy Acker, and the reviewer referred, dismissively I thought, to "Ackerish wailing and stamping." The reviewer was contrasting Acker's polyvalent texts that are performances of mimicry and, as Matias Viegener writes me yesterday, of patricide, with that of Chris Kraus's oeuvre, which the reviewer saw as able to explore more subtle spaces and textures than Acker's. Chris Kraus is my editor of the two books I've done with Semiotext(e), and an important writer for me, as is Kathy Acker. It always troubles me when, so often, two women writers are pitted against each other in the media, as if there's only one right way to be a writer or to write, which usually feels like the only mode that's right is the mode that's lyric, versus anti-lyric, that's poetic or meditative versus reactive and angry, etc. It has bothered me since I read it. But then I opened a page to Douglas Martin's new work about Acker, and here is Acker, in an interview with Sylvère Lotringer, "I act through the novels."

The above passage about the Greek-talking birds used to be in *Book of Mutter*, but I excised it. I believe that *Book of Mutter* used to read, in previous incarnations, as a gathering of different voices, of muttering, and madness, of acting through the book different monologues, more of, I guess one can say, a hysterical text. I am looking through edits that were from my manuscript on September 12, 2013, back when a poetry press was supposed to publish it. I was told at the time by the editor to take out anything that was too repetitive, too "cloying," and too "melodramatic." Which I think also meant—too hysterical. I was told this especially in a passage that dealt with nursing my dying mother—which reminds me as well of Anna O., the private theater of the griefstricken daughter. Although I resisted at the time, eventually I removed some of the repetitions, and eventually the text became less opaque, less of a private theater, and more controlled. I took out so much of the wailing and stamping out of the book on my mother. Again back to Woolf—the desire to write a controlled text, so as not to be misread.

I open up Anne Carson's essay "Gender of Sound," and see more underlinings, from my years of conceptualizing *Book of Mutter*.

> High vocal pitch goes together with talkativeness to characterize a person who is deviant from or deficient in the masculine ideal of self-control. Women, catamites, eunuchs and androgynes fall into this category. Their sounds are bad to hear and make men uncomfortable.

Anne Carson references the high-pitched and horrendous voices of the Furies, the babbling of Cassandra. The particular shriek of *oloyga*, issued forth in moments of ritualistic violence and childbirth. The ancients perceived something disorderly and deeply uncomfortable about female sound, which they allowed only to issue forth in ritualistic ways, such as the festival of *aishrologia*, or the ritual of saying ugly things, or, she writes, continuing to psychoanalysis, the cries of the hysteric. Both female sexuality and sound has been imagined as a leaky jar that needs to be contained.

> Woman is that creature who puts the inside on the outside. By projections and leakages of all kinds–somatic, vocal, emotional, sexual—females expose or expend what should be kept in.

Females blurt out a direct translation of what should be formulated indirectly.

This is in opposition to the masculine virtue of *sophrosyne*, or self-control, of which "verbal continence" is a major feature, which Carson reads as organizing patriarchal thought.

Recently I have been asked to do these talks at universities, and when I am brought in, I often feel I disappoint those who have asked me to speak, in terms of what I am thinking through now in my work. At one of the universities, I was asked beforehand to make sure to talk somehow about women, or feminism, as I was being co-sponsored by women's studies, and no doubt, Sofia writes me later, fulfilling some diversity requirement for university administration. I told them I was planning on delivering a talk on photography and Roland Barthes, but I'm imagining it would be somehow about women or feminism because a woman and a feminist would be delivering the talk, but I'm pretty sure that's not was meant. At the last talk, which was followed by a reading of my new work, a story about Franz Kafka, a student told me she was glad to hear me say that I was irritated in some ways by the hermit-bachelors I'm now writing through, by that tradition of male genius, in some ways like Woolf irritated by boys being allowed to learn Greek. She said in past work I was angry, and it didn't seem like in new work I was angry. She seemed disappointed by this. I told her not to worry, I was still often angry, and still felt often irritated. Afterwards, however, I felt disturbed by this question. In one way, I wonder whether I took out some of the anger in *Book of Mutter*, along with the high pitches and mutterings, in a desire to be not always such an irritant. I realized how influential the concept of the silent scream or the shriek was in previous work, but now I was exhausted, I was interested in other silences and spaces. "Why is female sound bad to hear?" Anne Carson asks in "Gender of Sound." When I was introduced by full-time faculty, both English professors who had done scholarship on *Heroines*, in these two talks, much was made of the fact that I do not have an MFA or a PhD, that I am not full-time faculty anywhere, and in some ways my work rankles and upsets traditional scholarship. Hearing this, I felt I had been asked to come in as an outsider, and produce the sounds that make others uncomfortable. Sofia reminds me, when I write this to her, that an adjunct is in a way an appendix. From the Latin it stems from *adjunctus*, or "closely connected, joined, united," but by the 1580s English adjunct meant "something added to but not an essential part of (something else)."

I remember when my first book *O Fallen Angel* came out, now almost a decade ago, a tacky theater of voices, how outside I felt from the coteries and communities of poetry. That I was supposed to be restrained, in my talk, not vulgar, ugly, angry, like the monologue of voices within my novel. After one of my first readings, which was with poets, on one of my first trips to New York as a published writer, a group of famous male poets were pointing and laughing at me at the bar afterwards, including a well-known translator of Maurice Blanchot, whose translations I very much admired. One of them, an editor of a Latin-American poetry anthology, came up to me, to the laughter of these other friends across the bar, and said to me, while gesturing at the translator, "My friend thinks you sound like an angry young woman. Are you an angry young woman?" It was clear that this much older man was mocking me, but he also seemed to be vaguely hitting on me, both forms of attention unwelcome and rather startling. Those I talked to about this afterwards were disturbed either of them would have said this to me—they are such supporters, they said, of women writers. You could tell they didn't really believe me, or thought I was making too much of something.

At the end of the essay "Gender of Sound," Anne Carson notes that she has often been called naïve in terms of bringing together different time periods and ethnographic sources in her work. It is my favorite part of the essay. She writes, "I think there is a place for naiveté in ethnography at the very least as an irritant." After this she writes that she has begun to question this Greek virtue of *sophrosyne*. She ends with: "I wonder if there might be another idea of human order than repression, another notion of human virtue than self-control, another kind of human self than one based on dissociation of inside and outside. Or indeed, another human essence than self." When I read this, I feel relieved somehow, like Anne Carson is giving me permission for these former drafts of my self, as well as for my current writing self, who desires multiplicity, who wants to write in different modalities, whether they be melancholy, exhaustion, irritation, anger, or joy, but not because it is expected of me. Which brings me back to the beginning—to Theresa Hak Kyung Cha's stuttering phrases, and to Anna O.'s cough. I still feel drawn to writing above all else that is in some ways an irritant.

Appendix F

ACCUMULATIONS

I've been keeping a mental list of all the pieces of art that I've nursed Leo in front of this past year. I remember at first, the two times I was out in public afterwards, both times at the Whitney, I was nervous to take my breast out, because Leo was crying and people were staring, I felt panicky and self-conscious, which I think made the baby more agitated. I became used to taking my breast out in art spaces, and began to savor it with sometimes a fatigued perversity and other times something more sacred, like the installation at the Lygia Pape show at the Met Breuer, in the corner of the nearly pitch-black room where gold thread made geometric curtains like beams of light, or recently on a bench in front of the El Greco Holy Family at the Met, the way in which Mary presses down on her breast and points the nipple towards baby Jesus, both her and Joseph gazing downwards at the central point of the baby, the baby's little hand on his mother's hand. I nursed Leo outside the bubblegum phallic Franz West sculpture at MASS MoCA, amidst the industrial landscape and gray cool light, her straddling me, downy head bobbing back and forth between each breast, and this fall in front of a Harry Dodge video at the New Museum's gender show, because there was a bench to sit on. I figured if there were so many penises in that room it was okay to have my breast peek out through my leather jacket, like a floppy blue-veined sac of a sculpture, scratched and sad. At the MOMA it is difficult to find a place to breastfeed. I didn't get to see all of the Louise Lawler show because it had taken all of our energy to get there on the subway, and it was almost closing time, and I couldn't find anywhere I felt comfortable to nurse, as the baby was still quite young and I still felt shaky and strange occupying public space in the city with a baby. A maintenance worker told me I could sit on the wooden pews in the atrium that were part of the exhibit, but the security guard told me I couldn't as I approached, and I apologized, but I kept on thinking that if Louise Lawler were there she probably would have let me breastfeed there, in the pews, because isn't her work about critiquing these institutional spaces? At the MOMA I've taken to nursing in the second floor lounge, outside the temporary gift shop, on one of the leather benches. I used to be so aware of people staring at me when I took my breast out, and I'm imagining they probably do look, as Leo is now almost a toddler, one year old this month, but I've stopped even thinking about someone staring at me, at least when with the baby, and there's a freedom to that. They might look at me but I don't look anymore at them looking at me. It's just the two of us, together.

As I'm writing this I get an email from Clutch, because I emailed them that I was looking at Catherine Opie's self-portrait of her breastfeeding her one-year-old baby, thinking how strange it was, that I was turning 40 next month and would have my first mammogram when my breasts were still full of milk—what a reminder of death and life at the same time, how much more can my body be wrung out and twisted—and that I planned to nurse Leo through the second year, even though I keep on being told I'm not going to feel like I have my body back until she weans. I don't know why I'm still nursing, it's something my body is doing and we do it together and it hasn't stopped yet, it's fluid, when it begins, when it ends, each session is fluid, and I feel time has been fluid, with the baby, there's no clear demarcations of boundaries, of time, our bodies, the self. What is a body, does one ever really get it back, that's what I wonder. This is something I know Clutch is interested in, transformations and time and the body. It turns out they had just shown the Opie photograph in their queer lit class, and all the students commented that the baby seemed too old, and Clutch had no idea, how to tell the age of babies, which I wouldn't have either, a year ago. I found it funny, the students' judgment about the maternal body, in a class on queerness. I wrote them that I loved how you can still see the scarring of Pervert across Opie's chest, from her previous self-portrait, something of how the body scars and bleeds, holds history and time, how even her breasts out reference her past work. How Opie is celebrating the postpartum body, the bigger, aching, drooping breast, held buoyant by her baby's mouth, echoing Renaissance poses, the smooth milk body of her toddler baby, curled into her capable tattooed arms. Something so permissive about that photo, that motherhood can be sweaty and tough and tender and yearning, and also that the artist was my age when she became pregnant, and it felt in opposition to her body and her life, at least to the outside world, to her gender presentation, to her subject matter as an artist, and that something transformative can come out of that contrariness. Also that she calls it a Self-Portrait, but there are two bodies in the photograph, the multiplicity of that identity, of early motherhood. I sent that same photograph to Suzanne, yesterday, and parroted her language from her last book. I want too to be punk about mothering, punk about aging, I wrote to Suzanne, quoting her. All I'm looking for lately are models of artists who have revolutionized their work as they get older, their hag years. I just sent Clutch and Suzanne a recent photograph I found online of Anne Carson at a reading, with these amazing yellow glasses, a plaid shirt, a leather jacket, and her gray hair held up with a schoolgirl red barrette and feeling mopey and weepy after a terrible haircut, thinking about my upcoming birthday. Her wrinkles like beautiful grooves in her face, like an etching. Have you ever seen a cooler bitch than this, I wrote them.

The photograph reminded me of the black-and-white Robert Mapplethorpe of Louise Bourgeois at about the same age, around 70, grinning in her black feather coat, a phallic sculpture tucked under one arm. Last week I went to see the retrospective of Louise Bourgeois's prints and books at the MOMA. The first in-person encounter I had with Louise Bourgeois's work was when I traveled to London to see the retrospective of her Cells which I realize is now a decade ago, for my 30th birthday, when she was still alive and making work. The next year we also went to New York, to the Guggenheim, to see her Cells again. Louise Bourgeois made 62 of these architectural spaces from 1991 to 2010, the year she died, I read in one of the MOMA placards. I am reminded again how Louise Bourgeois's work transformed as she got older, and she made some of her most significant work in the last two decades of her long life. When I first began to think about a Cell as a form, as an installation that's a room, I didn't vibrantly perceive as I do now the fact of her aging, that she is at the end of her life, and that she is storing in these Cells her objects and her memories, and that with Louise Bourgeois, the need to repeat these images and feelings and memories in the form of the objects she makes only intensifies over time. I guess I am thinking so much of her aging, and the passage of time in her work, because I am thinking of my own. Time has become the main object of contemplation for me, only intensified since I became a mother and as I am about to turn 40. There was one major Cell at the MOMA show, in the atrium on the second floor, a bronze Maman spider suspended over a cage, lined in fragments with an antique tapestry. The *Spider (Cell)* is from 1997. I walk around it, and think about how art is a container to hold and archive, and what it holds and archives is time. When I worked on the book about my mother, which I'm now realizing is not the only book on my mother, I began to think of a paragraph as a room or a cell. The paragraph also holds and contains time. I take notes on what's inside the Cell. Three glass jars hanging upside down in a row on one of the grates. A hanging sculpture. Little bones stuck in the cage's wire grates, tiny pendulums, a crystal from a chandelier, a hanging key, a perfume bottle, a hanging pocket watch. These items reminded me of my grandmother, who was Louise Bourgeois's age, the bureau in her bedroom upstairs, her watches and collection of perfume bottles. And also how just last week I found the bits I have of my mother's jewelry in a plastic bag tucked away in the pocket of an old suitcase. An inexpensive gold watch with a black face, a tiny gold topaz ring that only fit on my pinkie, as my fingers were still too swollen. I thought at the time how unsentimental I can be, about items like my mother's jewelry, yet how I hold fast to these objects in my memory, how smooth and cold her jewelry felt, her hands. I keep on circling around the Cell, going as close as the one of two security guards lets me, even though, as I read later, the Cell was originally meant to be sat inside, on the single chair in the center, covered in a tattered tapestry. You are meant to go within and sit on the chair and be under the mother spider's protection. That the Cell holds two meanings, as does the mother as spider—as a form of protection and then also a prison-like enclosure.

The space where the *Spider (Cell)* sits is surrounded by very tall black and white etchings that Louise Bourgeois made in her 90s, with titles like *Accumulations* and *The Fall* and *Losing It* and *The Unfolding*. These vertical sketches that are accumulations, images of increasing multiplicity, of looping towers of bulbs, breasts, leaves, eggsacs. How Louise Bourgeois has theorized that the vertical is active, an attempt to escape, unlike the horizontal, which is passive, wanting to go to bed. How hanging and floating are states of ambivalence. In one of the etchings, in a series named after a Balzac heroine, she has handwritten phrases about daily life and housework: "I have spent my life washing dishes and vegetables—I have spent my life listening to the chirping of birds—the water dripping from the ceiling—I have spent my life smelling the burning from the stove." I forgot, staring at the handwriting on that etching, how much I was influenced by Louise Bourgeois's writings, even the appearance of her handwriting. As I stood there with the stroller, my baby's red shoes dangling, it came over me with such a wave of intensity and feeling, the monumentality of this artist with three sons, how I had completely omitted this before when thinking of her work. And how, to extend this, I completely did not grasp the monumentality of my mother with three small children, when I wrote a book about her, over those years. I had always thought of Louise Bourgeois as mourning her childhood and her mother in her later work, but how she too was a mother, how so much of the mother grows and needles into her work, the drawings and prints especially. How she began to think towards her mother even as an older woman, how time became layered. Standing in front of that etching I witnessed a conversation between three older women, one woman in her 90s in a wheelchair being pushed by another woman. Is this your mother? the woman asks the woman pushing the wheel-chair. When she says yes, the woman says to her, in that conversational New York way, "Well I hope you don't think of your own mother as a spider." And then they have a rather unpleasant conversation (to me) arguing about the mental wellness of such an obsessive artist. If I felt like talking to them, I would have told them that Louise Bourgeois's mother was a seamstress, and the spider is a mostly positive, however ambivalent, image for her. Her spiders in drawings and much later in sculptures as pairs, tiny crawling on walls, like in that room, nesting in families. The Cell in the room where we are standing in is the web that the spider encloses and protects. I read from an interview with Bourgeois: "The spider…why the spider? Because my best friend was my mother and she was deliberate, clever, patient, soothing, reasonable, dainty, subtle, indispensable, neat and useful as a spider." I say to Leo, It's a spider!, as her favorite song is The Itsy Bitsy Spider, which I sing to her on trains and airport lines, whenever she's antsy in public, which used to work but really has stopped, and there's also a book about a busy spider that she likes. Later all three women come up to the baby and the stroller and coo at her and talk to her.

All day as I write this I am on the couch, thinking about Louise Bourgeois, weepy and exhausted from too much teaching, too little sleep, still depressed over my bad haircut. John brings the baby to me, as she nurses, in increasingly acrobatic positions suspended over me. I think of how I can work on these sketches when I can't do anything else, when I am too sad and exhausted. Can writing follow a sort of verticality, sentences and thoughts held in suspension? My favorite prints from the show are *The Fragile*, the series of 36 compositions on fabric, Louise Bourgeois made the drawings at 95 years old while sitting in bed, a series of self-portraits from youth to old age, all about motherhood and the metamorphosis of the maternal body, massive drooping breasts, as if the body was made entirely of breasts, spiders, other bulbous bodies. Her drawings and prints are often about the elastic female body, the dissembling of the body in childbirth and nursing and motherhood, its multiplicity and monstrosity. At the show I watch the video of her first fabric book, from 2002, *Ode à l'oubli*, or *Ode to Forgetting*, made of the worn linen hand towels saved from her wedding trousseau. I watch her turn each page and smooth them with her hand, covered in liver spots, her wedding ring, there was something of how she smoothes the page, like she is folding one of the napkins, that deliberate and almost automatic gesture that reminded me of my grandmother again, those decades working in linens at Marshall Field's, the same smoothing motion of her hand across a set of sheets. It is a domestic gesture but also an artistic one. The folding over of the page, a going over images in the past, a rewriting and rethinking. In her 80s Louise Bourgeois decided she didn't need to save her clothes or fabrics so she placed the Clothes suspended in her Cells and cut up the fabrics for her books and stuffed heads and figures. She didn't need to hold onto her sacred objects she stored for so many years, she realized that a way to actually store them was to put them in her work. There's something so intimate and visceral about this, this reusing and repeating, the way her work holds the past, her memories, what it wrings through and contains.

Appendix G

STILLS/FACES

On my 40th birthday I am on the couch looking at Marguerite Duras's Wikipedia page. I read that she wrote *Hiroshima mon amour* and *Ravishing Lol Stein* in her mid-forties, and this makes me feel calmer. My daughter Leo is making ecstatic and sometimes pained sounds with her father in the kitchen—their morning routine of watching the feral cats eating the food John leaves outside of the window. She wakes up concerned about the cats. Maybe she wonders why they are outdoors and not inside, like us. How enraptured I've become by my baby's open, ferocious face. It's everything that is beautiful to me. Sometimes she will kiss me suddenly, our teeth clashing, other times she will hit me repeatedly in the face, laughing. She's lazing on the floor now, sucking her pacifier and doing pelvic thrusts, her sleepy pre-nap exercise. Today for the first time I saw her offer her face for the dog to kiss, which he did, repeatedly. She's spinning around and around, doing her sleepy walk, as the dog watches her. It is snowing. I watch it. Our tiny Christmas tree is still up. Everything slows until John and I can make notes in the near dark, during her sleep.

The entire past year I have been writing these series of texts, so often in the dark while my baby sleeps. There is something fitting about this, to be almost in the dark while tracing through the shadow of the book on my mother, that I worked on for a decade, begun so soon after her death, and that I only finished in the early weeks of being pregnant with Leo. Something uncanny about this, my new solitude that I write to, always doubled, even though she sleeps. That these appendices, thinking about what I failed at or omitted in *Book of Mutter*, or want to continue writing through, are the new container in which I can put my memories, and by that I mean my ongoing grief. How they have marked time for me, over this year.

If I begin to write something today I can be reminded again of how a text can mark time. How a painting can do this also—*I worked on this painting today*. I am now reading about the South African painter Marlene Dumas. Dumas thought the speed of a work was important—her paintings that often remain closer to drawings, with their sources found in photographs and film stills. But she says somewhere that the meaning of a painting is not where it begins, or where it ends, but somewhere between the beginning and the end, for therein lies the shadow. When working on the book about my mother I often stared at an image of Dumas's painting of the recently dead Marilyn Monroe, painted from a photograph from her autopsy. Autopsy comes from the Greek: *to see with one's own eyes*. I had seen the painting in a show of Marlene Dumas, I believe in New York, a decade ago, when I was working on the book. There was something about the gestures of the painting and its coloration that reminded me of Francis Bacon's painting of William Blake's life mask, but this is like a death mask. I remember being moved by Dumas's icy blues, something shocking about making beautiful Marilyn's puffy and bruised face, making beautiful this deeply upsetting photograph, of such a life force in movies now dead and decaying (a contrast with how Warhol painted an endless emptiness of Marilyn's almost clownish grin from the *Niagara* publicity still).

Previous versions of the book on my mother included a passage in which I detailed the room in which Marilyn Monroe was found dead, on the evening of August 4, 1962. How she had retreated to the bedroom with her telephone. How she must have dragged the long extension cord down the hallway into the bedroom. How she made a number of calls, including one to the movie actor Peter Lawford. How she called her hairdresser to schedule an appointment. How she was found the next morning by police completely naked, face down, positioned diagonally across her bed, still holding the telephone. How around 10pm her live-in housekeeper had said that she walked past the door and saw a light underneath but decided not to disturb her. How at midnight she says she saw the light again and called Marilyn's psychiatrist. How the psychiatrist claims he tried to break through the door but failed. How when interviewed he stated that he saw Marilyn lying there holding the telephone through the French windows outside so then smashed them in. How there were dark curtains covering the windows. How when the police sergeant arrived the housekeeper had been doing laundry and cleaning. How the bed had fresh linen on it. How when questioned she said that she wanted the place to look nice. How this was the one room Marilyn didn't allow her to enter. All of which I excised in the final version—including more about the sadness of her life and the spectacle of suspicion surrounding her death—although there are ghostly fragments that remain.

I couldn't remember why I felt compelled to juxtapose these scenes of Marilyn Monroe's death and myth in a book about my mother, what that original impulse was, or why I wanted to include portraits of the isolation and death of Joan of Arc, or actresses such as Renee Falconetti, playing Joan of Arc, or Barbara Loden or Joan Crawford. And yet I read recently that Marlene Dumas painted *Dead Marilyn* in 2008 as a response to her mother's death the year before, also out of an inability to finish the painting of her mother that she had been working on. I want to understand why Marlene Dumas painted *Dead Marilyn* as opposed to her mother, as a way through her grief. The abstraction of the faces of the film stills and fallen stars that Dumas painted in that year, the year after her mother's death, as opposed to the painting of her mother, that she could not complete. *For Whom the Bell Tolls*, an extreme close-up of the face of Ingrid Bergman, her face layered with tears, so that her skin appears pink-warped and burned. Emmanuelle Riva's face in *Hiroshima mon amour*. A still most likely from when she is in bed, her gaze intense with remembering. Yet in the painting the face of the woman looks burned or fallen or dead, perhaps texturally mixing the sweat of the lovers with the ashes and disfigured skin of the victims of the atomic bombing shown at the beginning of the film, these victims the white French woman wants so desperately to empathize with, to merge her own personal devastation of wartime with their horror. Perhaps Dumas was trying to think of her mother when painting these actresses in film stills playing characters who are individuals trapped in history, wrestling with personal experiences of grief, characters who are also actresses, like Emmanuelle Riva in *Hiroshima mon amour*, who is filming a peace film in Hiroshima. Perhaps the painter's sadness mourning her mother, a white woman raising children in rural South Africa during apartheid, was too complicated, mixed in with what comes through in other work, grief and guilt as to the painter's role in history and her country's collective past of colonialism and violence (her self-portrait entitled *Evil is Banal*, that ambiguous gaze).

Dumas's painting of Renee Falconetti's Joan of Arc in *Sleeping with the Enemy*, also cadaver-like, like so many of Dumas's close-ups. How her canvases can become coffins for her figures. Dumas has explained with this series of crying women that images of sadness are often in film but rarely in contemporary painting. There is something private and opaque about these paintings. Also, when watching these actresses on screen we can only imagine their interiority. *What makes you so sad?*, Clark Gable asks Marilyn Monroe's character in *The Misfits*, as he/we take in the blank beauty of her face, her head reclined back. *I think you're the saddest girl I've ever met.*

I want to think about images of sadness that we borrow from. Marlene Dumas's series of crying women in cinema reminds me of that moment near the beginning of Claudia Rankine's *Don't Let Me Be Lonely*, when the speaker visits the Museum of Emotions in London, and is supposed to answer Yes or No to the question in an installation: "Were you terribly upset and did you find yourself weeping when Princess Diana died?" The speaker steps on the tile for "No" and is not allowed to continue the quiz. She then wonders if Princess Diana was ever really alive to anyone outside of those who knew her. Perhaps mourning her death was in some way a projection. A still from a TV, the thousands of mourners leaving flowers in front of the palace. Rankine writes, "Weren't they mourning the protection they felt she should have had? A protection they'll never have? Weren't they simply grieving the random inevitability of their own deaths?"

These blocks of texts like film stills or the static of TV screens. A contemplative space to gaze into. In both Dumas's paintings and Rankine's text, a repository of constant images from the media. The speaker sits in her room and watches TV. An early memory of watching movies as a child, and always wondering if the actor on the screen is now dead. "The years went by and people only died on television—if they weren't Black, they were wearing black or were terminally ill." She feels oversaturated by a collective grief, what she sees through the screen, black men murdered or beaten by police, the events of 9/11. National images of mourning. Which reminds me of Marlene Dumas's series of African women whose husbands were assassinated or were political prisoners—like her paintings of Pauline Lumumba, inspired by that newspaper photograph of her walking through the street, chest ritualistically bared, mourning her slain husband, the former prime minster of the Republic of Congo.

Don't Let Me Be Lonely is like a museum of sadness, both private and collective. In the first passage, a block of text in its own page/wall, like an installation, two layered childhood memories, her mother's stillbirth when the speaker was 8, and her father sitting on a stoop outside, his face leaking, as his mother had just died. The book begins, "There was a time I could say no one I knew well had died. This is not to suggest no one died." These juxtaposed portraits of private grief—the speaker's depression, her sister's tragic loss of her entire family in a car crash, a friend dying of breast cancer, another friend's diagnosis of Alzheimer's, another friend's even more severe depression. In that scene, the speaker narrates going over to her friend's house, where they watch Werner Herzog's *Fitzcarraldo*. As they watch the film her friend begins weeping. A still of Klaus Kinski. The next section/installation, after a blank page and another blank page, with an illustration of the static of a TV screen, an image of Timothy McVeigh's empty electric chair (recalling Warhol?), a consideration of Jacques Derrida's writings on forgiveness. The speaker decides that forgiveness is not a form of madness, as Derrida claims, but instead a sort of death. "It is a feeling of nothingness that cannot be communicated to another, an absence, a bottomless vacancy held by the living, beyond all that is hated or loved."

A large bouquet of pale pink and white roses from my sister comes to the door. They are almost frozen. Later, peach roses from John. Did someone die? I joke. My sister texts me, when I thank her for the flowers, that she thinks her husband is leaving her. I go on their Instagram page—he is almost erased. Only smiling faces on Instagram. And for my sister, to me, as well, even with this news, always smiley emoticons. My sister hidden and private, like our mother was. Or perhaps she buries these feelings down and refuses them. Or perhaps just refuses them to me, I don't know. I forgot in the Rankine, although I've read it many times before, that she writes of turning 40 towards the end, receiving lilies from her parents. How strange that I am to reread it today, how I reached for it, from the top of the couch, it was just sitting there on the bookshelf. "It occurs to me that forty could be half my life or it could be all my life," she writes.

I remember now, when my mother turned 40, her friends threw her an Over the Hill party. The black balloons buoyed to the ceiling of our basement. She received a birthday card that described what the day was like in New York, the day she was born. All her life her mother, who she was estranged from, had told her that she gave birth on Thanksgiving, and had to miss Thanksgiving dinner, and how upset she was by this. But it turns out, she wasn't born on Thanksgiving. My mother was furious. I wrote this all in the book on my mother, but took it out, I don't know why. It felt silly, maybe. Or it wasn't my memory, but what my father, later, reported to me. My mother with all of her secrets. I go back to the beginning of *Don't Let Me Be Lonely*, the mother returning home from the hospital without a baby. The memory of her mother's seeming nonchalance versus her father's weeping face. "Did she shrug? She was the kind of woman who liked to shrug; deep within her was an everlasting shrug." Two years later Dumas finished the painting of her mother, which was painted from a photograph of her mother as a girl (*My moeder voor sy my moeder was*, or *My mother before she was my mother*, a Barthesian construct). A young woman in white, waving, her face white, blurred, ghostly, against a background of gold. Of her mother, Rankine writes, "She wants me to lead a readable life—one that can be read as worthwhile, and successful." A readable life. Is that the same as a writable one?

I read the dedication to Rankine's book—I realize it's to her daughter, who it seems she was pregnant with while finishing the book in her 40th year. She doesn't mention pregnancy or birth in the book. The extreme intimacy and yet opacity of the speaker. And yet does the work exist in this postpartum space, something of its grief and exhaustion, its porousness? A book becomes of its time, the body in the room in the act of composition, and somehow out of its time. Between the two is the shadow.

Appendix H

STILLS/ROOMS

"I read many books about people sitting in rooms, and these were all by writers I knew."— Renee Gladman, *Calamities*

I want to begin with the inwardness of a cork-filled room. In *The Preparation of the Novel*, the series of lectures given at the end of his life, Roland Barthes conjures up Marcel Proust's address at 102 Boulevard Hausmann, where the asthmatic writer enclosed himself into his rear-facing room, that he secured from the outside world, from noise and dust and cooking smells. It was here, for over a decade, that he wrote *In Search of Lost Time*, this period of what Barthes calls Proust's *Vita Nova*, his new practice of writing catalyzed by his mother's death, Proust here a double for Barthes's longings.

It was in this room with the heavy blue satin curtains that Proust could go entirely into his past. Barthes describes how, regardless of the temperature, Proust would light a fire, and cover himself with three hot water bottles, seven woolen blankets, and a fur coat. Here, in the

Talk given at CalArts, March 5, 2018

lecture notes, Barthes makes a distinction between writing from the bed and writing from the desk. Perhaps, he theorizes, writing from the desk is "careful, well-thought-through, difficult" and writing that issues forth from the bed is "hurried, flowing, spontaneous."

As I work on this talk, I am on the couch, again, my baby asleep on a pillow next to me. A couch is more like a bed than a desk, and mine is always covered with pillows, blankets, various books. I am, as usual while writing these appendices this past year, hunched over, with terrible posture, in the dark, with the same trance-like music as my accompaniment, the setting in which we try to create night during the day for my daughter. This is the atmospheric interiority in which I now enter the space of this text, which will reside in a series of rooms, of people alone in rooms, of rooms alone.

Somewhat appropriately, I have been laid up with chest pain, possibly the result of lifting my daughter repeatedly or letting her sprawl heavily across my chest while I feed her in the middle of the night. I went to urgent care, sure that I was having a heart attack, that I was dying, another reminder for me lately of the translucent skin that divides the ordinary day from the certainty of our mortality. I am supposed to sleep, as I have not been getting much sleep lately, but instead I take notes.

I think I finally understand why in the lectures Barthes begins with the small form of the haiku. The haiku marks the cellular beginnings of his desire for the novel, which parallels his desire to make a narrative out of the present. The haiku, he writes, is a philosophy of the instant. The "surprise of a *gesture*." I think to that moment in Sophie Calle's *Address Book*, when she visits Pierre D's apartment, knowing he is absent, and drags her hand slowly into his mailbox, across his unopened letters. The tenderness of such a gesture.

Could a work be composed of such small forms, gestures and sentences, with, as Barthes writes, the "ascetic, elliptical workings" of a haiku? He quotes Valéry on "the essential thinness of things."

In his *Mourning Diary*, haiku-like slivers of the present tense of grief, of the moment of writing.

In Barthes's grief diary, he repeatedly conjures up the space in which he's writing. On the entry of October 31: "Monday, 3pm. Back alone for the first time in the apartment. How am I going to manage to live here all alone? And at the same time, it's clear there's no other place." The "here" is the empty apartment that he once shared with his mother, that shared space of grief where she still lingers, but it is also the empty page, where he now resides.

This is also why he's so interested in the space where Proust is writing his memories—that it was an apartment known by Proust's mother, that he can inhabit the intensity of this physical space to go back to the past. Is this why Barthes's title in French for his book on photography, which is his book searching after the ghost photograph of his mother, is *La Chambre Claire*? The space of grief and the space of the page is an empty room.

Can I extend Heidegger's question in his lecture, "Building, Dwelling, Thinking": not only, what is it to dwell, but what is it to dwell in grief? And when was it that I realized that these appendices were rooms where I still dwelled within my grief?

I am interested in the book as a space, and what happens within this space, what becomes transformed in terms of grief and time. In Claudia Rankine's *Don't Let Me Be Lonely*, the blocks of texts like the privacy of rooms. So much of the text takes place in bedrooms, where family members and friends are ill and dying, or have died. The speaker sits on the edge of the bed. The TV always flickers in the background. Sometimes a movie is on. People are dying or have died there as well.

The way solitude is felt within Rankine's work, much like in Barthes's grief diary. Something of the numb tone feels spatial. It takes up residence within us, the reader. For there is also the room, in which the reader is reading, the deep interiority and insulation of the text.

How a life can be sliced open, in a sudden change of the everyday. I have been in too many hospitals and doctor's offices lately. About a month ago, as I'm thinking through this talk, my daughter has an accident on the playground. A man, one of the fathers, ran into her. He didn't see her, toddling about. There is something so banal—I repeat to myself, a dull recitation—my baby had an accident on the playground, a man ran into her. She had to be rushed to the emergency room, she has countless stitches on a wound on her face…although this conveys nothing.

When I tell it this way it feels too detached—although that's what language feels like it has to be now, like a report. The exhaustion of caretaking and witness. To write of grief, which is to write of solitude, is to write the banal details of a life. On October 29 of Barthes's *Mourning Diary*: "In taking these notes, I'm entrusting myself to the *banality* that is in me."

When I get the call from John—our child has had an accident—I should come to the playground as soon as possible. As soon as I hear this—our child has had an accident—I drop the phone and run out without a coat, in the cold, several city blocks, gathering her in my arms, collapsing on the sidewalk outside of the coffee shop, nursing my baby as she bleeds all over me. In that moment of the phone call I had actually been reading Blanchot on "Everyday Speech," trying to prepare for this talk. Take her to the playground, I had said, I need some time to think.

Blanchot writes, "The everyday is platitude (what lags and falls back, the residual life with which our trash cans and cemeteries are filled: scrap and refuse); but this banality is also what is most important, if it brings us back to existence in its very spontaneity and as it is lived-in-the-moment, when lived, it escapes every speculative formulation, perhaps all coherence, all regularity." (This is from a translation by Susan Hanson.)

Birth, death, accidents—all so everyday. The everyday is who we are, "ourselves, ordinarily."

Peter Handke's *A Sorrow Beyond Dreams*, his book unraveling his mother's life and suicide, shares something of the detached, exhausted tone of the mourning diaries of Rankine and Barthes. Like a report or an investigation, it is an attempt to read his mother's life. What he can gather is everyday facts, like objects. The post-office receipt for a registered letter found in her pocket.

Handke performs here language's inability to communicate horror or grief. In these notes written over two months, we can sense the body writing in the room. We are told, at the end, that he will write about it in greater depth elsewhere—his own speechlessness fighting against the speechlessness of his mother's existence.

He sets forth to collect the lean facts of her life—a woman born in the same small Austrian village where she died, with only a brief interlude in the city, before the war. A claustrophobic interiority to the book to mirror his mother's extreme interiority. The monotony of time passing.

A section on the weather in Barthes's lectures on the novel, continuing his thinking through the haiku. He notes how the French word for weather —*temps*—is the same as time. The weather has "an *existential* charge; it brings the subject's *feeling-being* into play, the pure and mysterious sensation of life." Handke too writes to his mother's claustrophobic interiority within the house. The longing and limit of windows.

> "Rain—sun; outside—inside: feminine feelings were very much dependent on the weather, because 'outside' was seldom allowed to mean anything but the yard and 'inside' was invariably the house, without a room of one's own."

Thinking through these texts lately, of still rooms and grief, I have wondered—what if when we are describing a text, we describe somehow its weather?

When we talk about my daughter's wound, we have stopped saying "scar," because she knows what we're talking about. We instead speak about the "garden." "How is the garden, do you think it's looking better today?"

Handke's speculative tone. His lists—his capitalizations and exclamations—like a breathless monologue but delivered in a detached style. The intrusions and internalizing of his mother's voice.

> "City life: short skirts ('knee huggers'), high-heeled shoes, permanent wave, earrings, unclouded joy of life. Even a stay abroad! Chambermaid in the Black Forest, flocks of ADMIRERS, kept at a DISTANCE!"

A girl taken in by the parade of Nazism. We are told, in a sentence with remarkable ambiguity and restraint, his mother's voice filtered through the author-narrator's horror, that Hitler had a nice voice on the radio. Then marriage, children, the war, the return home. To be inside again. A parataxis much like through the Kentucky scenes in Elizabeth Hardwick's *Sleepless Nights*, a display of the rigid economy of a life.

> "Was there, then, nothing more? Had that been all? Masses for the dead, childhood diseases, drawn curtains, correspondence with old acquaintances of carefree days, making herself useful in the kitchen and in the fields, running out now and then to move the child into the shade, then, even here in the country, air-raid sirens, the population scrambling into the cave shelters, the first bomb crater, later used for children's games and as a garbage dump."

Handke's still but moving portrait of his mother, now a housewife. The exhausting monotony and isolation of her life. The litany of shame in rural Germany. The misery of a loveless marriage. The line where we are told that she gave herself an abortion with a knitting needle, a sentence itself like a needle.

A series of lists and parentheticals like rosary beads. The dull monotony of the recitation. "The trivia of daily life." Like the prose equivalent of Chantal Akerman's Jeanne Dielman peeling potatoes. A stingy domesticity. An eternity of housework. The constant repetition: "...folding, unfolding; emptying, filling; plugging in, unplugging. 'Well, that does it for today.'" All of the listings, of objects in the room, objects used and put back, returned to their place.

The unraveling when his mother, in her despair, suddenly stopped her daily chores. He describes her wandering listlessly about the house. Not being able to follow the endless parade of her television. The voice of her letters to the narrator begin to filter through at the end, the facts of a day belying desperation and isolation, recalling how a young Chantal Akerman reads her mother's assumedly unanswered letters in News from Home.

To open Elizabeth Hardwick's Sleepless Nights is to enter the room of the writer writing, and the writer remembering. The book begins in the interior of the writer-narrator, the apartment she inhabits alone. The mise-en-scène of a life: "Every morning the blue clock and the crocheted bedspread with its pink and blue and gray squares and diamonds. How nice it is—this production of a broken old woman in a squalid nursing home."

The narrator in Sleepless Nights surrounds herself with objects, and memory appears as cans on a shelf, as she sits in a room, writing, which is remembering. One can is marked her childhood address in Kentucky, and if she chooses to take it down from the shelf, inside will be the "blackening porches of winter, the gas grates, the swarms." The narrator moves in and out of the past, to various addresses. Always at first the set decoration in letters to "M." A tableau of interiors. The windows and rooms. Boston 1954. The weather. "I am looking out on a snowstorm." The lists of winter costumes she watches from the street. The house with four floors. "Flowered curtains made to measure, rugs cut for the stairs, bookshelves, wood for the fireplace."

As I work on this talk in various rooms, the objects that surround me. On the floor, broken crayons and torn out sheets of blank paper with spare squiggles; board books; wooden pegs; the tiny colorful xylophone with the wooden hammer repurposed to bang on it; blocks; various stuffed animals, differentiated by how much our dog is allowed to chew on them; small errant puzzle pieces we have given up collecting at the end of the night; the fuzz escaping from the rugs; books and notebooks on tops of couches and on various desks and tables; student essays; coffee cups and water glasses; discarded robes and cardigans; piled-up boxes from things ordered online.

It takes me several days to watch Chantal Akerman's last film, *No Home Movie*, a film that takes place almost entirely in her elderly mother's Brussels apartment, before her mother's death. I have been putting it off for more than a year, since Chantal Akerman's sudden death, although I have rewatched many of her earlier films several times since then, always pausing, taking notes. I think I was afraid it would open up something inside me, several layers of grief, and in her way, make me still—dwell—with my thoughts and memories in a way that I had not wished to return to.

Four minutes and 28 seconds—I measure the opening long shot of the violent thrashing of trees with the wind, the cars in the distance.

Like a barely moving landscape painting. From Rankine's *Don't Let Me Be Lonely*, describing the outside view from the room that the speaker's severely depressed friend doesn't leave: "The leaves on the tree outside his window rattled within him."

Except for these interludes outside, we are inside for most of the film, inside like Natalia Akerman, who we first see from behind, frail, in a white sweater, black slacks, and house slippers, opening a door and slowly moving into the pink and mauve interior of the dining room that we've been contemplating.

Time passes in the Akerman style. We get to know each room, its heavy interiors. These almost static shots. Like Vermeer paintings— the same room, with the windows. How Akerman marks day and night in a stasis of one location (a hotel in *Hotel Monterey*, a room in the first part of *Je tu il elle*, a Brussels apartment). The changes of light and passing of time. The potted trees against the translucent curtains. The rugs. The geometry of the cabinets. The clutter and fragility, the lived-in-ness. All of these *things*. I keep on pausing and making lists of the objects in the frame.

In the kitchen, the mother and daughter sit and eat potatoes, a nod to *Jeanne Dielman*. Also in the kitchen, later, the daughter tries to get her mother to talk, about her escape from Poland, about the camps, the same story repeated, like gossip almost, the need to hear the conversation, the need to repeat. A layered space in the kitchen— past films, past conversations.

One slowly realizes, watching this, that the mother rarely leaves her apartment. The slow way in which she gathers up her purse, towards the end of the film, to take a walk around the block with her aide. The memory of my grandmother in her house, then my uncle, her son, both in that reading chair, dully watching television, as they were in decline. How much energy it took my mother to leave the house, when she was sick.

The feel of time passing, so beautiful and banal. To think about a life and its confines. How can writing approach this space of contemplation. How to represent privacy and sadness in a work. The daughter is the camera. The camera is the daughter. I sense the grieving daughter, editing this work, pausing, watching her mother in decline. Her presence and then her absence.

The scene towards the end of the film that so devastated me it took me forever to watch it, as I kept on pausing, getting up, continuing my day, going back to the screen. Up at night, the daughter begins to film, the rain outside on the balcony, the empty cars on the street, the inhabited bathroom, its sogginess, the two robes hanging, one pale blue one navy blue, the lotions and towels. The strange light of the night. An extended shot of the geometry of the bathroom door, a typical minimal Akerman composition. The grid of checked towels hanging on the clothesline against the light. The mother coughing in the dark. We only hear her. The sound of fear and fatigue in the old woman's voice. The daughter calls her mommy.

I remember, watching this, my aunt and grandmother sharing a bed together, whispering to each other, my grandmother's moans of pain in the night. My own memories as well of caretaking, this small world, where everything becomes a room or series of rooms.

That devastating moment in *Mourning Diary*:

October 27.
Every morning, around 6:30, in the darkness outside, the metallic racket of the garbage cans.

She would say, with relief: the night is finally over (she suffered during the night, alone, a cruel business).

The enormity of this night sequence in Akerman's film—I want to write an entire novel inside of it, and I only have these notes. I want to leave thinking about the gaze of witnessing someone else alone in a room, at once invasive and tender. The gaze of writing of one's person who cannot sleep, up in the middle of the night. There is such an intimacy in imagining an interiority. The rooms within them. The rooms within us.

Appendix I

TYPES OF VESTIGIAL STRUCTURES

A man came up to me after the last talk that I gave, when interviewing for a full-time teaching job, which I didn't get. He was a scientist at the school, he explained, and he thought it was interesting to think about the appendix, in a biological sense, in the context of my project. We think of the appendix as the vestigial structure in the human body, having lost its original function or perhaps having evolved, but, this man asked me, had I heard of the *cecum*? I knew vaguely that it connected to something dealing with the large intestine. He told me to go home and look it up, as I might find rich the metaphysical implications of its original purpose, which I am doing now. In the digestive tracts of herbivores, the cecum stores the bacteria which is able to break down the cellulose in plants. In humans, the cecum has an outmoded purpose—it no longer serves as a site of cellulose digestion, like it did for our ancestors—it is simply a small pouch forming part of the large intestine. Both the cecum and the appendix no longer have much of a purpose in human beings, except that they can be inflamed, and then need to be removed. The name derives from the Latin "caecum," or "blind"—literally a dead-end or cul-de-sac. I wonder if I can think of this small text as a cecum instead of an appendix—a dead-end pouch, a cul-de-sac wherein I circle blindly? Used to have a purpose. Vulnerable to being inflamed and then will have to be removed.

All morning I lounge in bed, drinking coffee, as I was up late at night, overcome with grief. Yesterday was March 17, which is the official date the coroner listed as my mother's date of death, now 16 years ago. It is also one year since I began working on these appendices, this cul-de-sac to my mourning. I haven't done much to observe the anniversary this year. I didn't even call my father, which I usually do. I wonder if that's what really got to me, as I laid there in bed, unable to sleep. In the years since her death, I would always have *Book of Mutter* to work on, a ritual, to at least open and reread, and this past year I've had this project. And now even this vestigial project is over, or almost over. Last night I tried to remember my mother, not the ways I've written about her, not her on her deathbed, but her, who she was, and who she was as my mother, and what it felt like, to have a mother, to be mothered, and I found it difficult. Some collage of gestures, and the textures of her clothes, and the feel of her skin, and things she would say, and moments of being with her flitted through my consciousness, the years all mixed up, but I couldn't focus on anything. I felt somehow last night that I had lost her again, and I wondered whether that would happen to me, whether someday my daughter would have to squeeze her eyes shut, at night in bed in her middle-age, and try to conjure up something of my presence. How long I've meditated upon my mother's absence. And what now, I wonder, nothing? Which felt like another sort of death. I felt a sharp feeling in my chest, a pressure that only could release if I could weep, not in the brief, almost voluptuous way I've allowed myself to feel pain lately, like the full-body aura of disappointment a few days ago, learning that I was not going to be offered the job I spent two months interviewing for and preparing for and exhausting myself over, having just recovered from traveling to California and back in two days with my baby and my partner, or the anxiety and dread I have tried to tamper down upon learning about car crashes and school shootings and nanny trials, everything in the news, all my fears about death and mortality, mostly focused on my child. Perhaps it was all mixed in there—the pain, the panic, the disappointment and worry—with the shudders of my weeping. We heard the baby howling in the next room—and John went and got her for me. He wondered whether somehow she heard her mother, or sensed I needed her. I cradled her and soothed her and kissed her wet face. I thought about my mother, how much I'm sure she held me as a baby, even though it is impossible to remember, like it will be impossible for Leo to remember. Afterwards, I felt something like a release and was able to sleep, and now, I'm up, eyes swollen, writing. I'm realizing lately that writing for me is a form of resilience. That whenever I'm sad, or grieving, I need to write something to commemorate it, and try to turn it into something to think through, something hopefully profound. The vestigial remnants of my resilience, my existence.

Appendix J

STUTTERS OF HISTORY

In the book on my mother, I removed several threads that dealt with history, usually American history. I now don't remember clearly what remains in the published book and what exists instead in the ghostly space of the archive. I don't completely understand why I devoted so much space for example to the disintegration of Mary Todd Lincoln in previous drafts. She still exists, in remnants, in the book on my mother as it was published. Mary Todd Lincoln is something of a ghost in the book, a persisting image of the grieving widow in black Victorian mourning silks visiting William Mumler's studio, the ghostly fiction of her slain husband hovering over her. I've often been drawn to repulsive women who, through being demonized, have acquired the status of myth in literature and history, perhaps especially American literature and history. In an interview published at the end of her collection on archives and early Americana, *The Birth-mark*, Susan Howe says: "It's the stutter in American literature that interests me. I hear the stutter as a sounding of uncertainty. What is silenced or not quite silenced. All the broken dreams." I believe that through the process of writing this book on my mother I was attempting to write something of this stutter, what I called mutter, and that was the rhythm of how I composed, at my desk, and on the floor, cutting up strips of paper and moving them around.

I began working on the book on my mother in the summer of 2007, soon after attending an exhibit entitled "Mary Todd Lincoln: First Lady of Controversy" at the Lincoln Museum in Springfield, Illinois. The scene of visiting the exhibit on Mary Todd Lincoln still remains within the published book, although somewhat mysteriously, as most of the material dealing with the Lincolns was otherwise removed. One of the reasons I attended the exhibit was because I had followed my partner John to the University of Illinois at Urbana-Champaign, for his required summer residency for a graduate library program, and, having nothing to do during the day except work in a coffeeshop, I wanted to take a road trip. The capital of Illinois was nearby, which evoked strange memories for me of childhood trips. My father and his identical twin, my now deceased-uncle, were obsessed with all things American history, particularly American presidential and military history, and especially the history of Illinois. I don't know what made my father and his brother so obsessed with Civil War battlefields and presidential homes and libraries, visits to which structured our summer vacations. Or why the Chicago outsider artist Henry Darger and his father were also similarly obsessed. Was this some sort of boyish obsession, growing up in Illinois, a pride at Illinois's native son, Abraham Lincoln? My father and uncle both served as officers in the Navy, having begun ROTC while attending Northwestern University, and both having served on aircraft carriers in wartime, which I only discovered while my uncle was dying. Sitting in my grandmother's rocking chair in the living room in the old Oak Park house, my grandmother having died a couple years earlier, my uncle would tell us stories of his youth, including how my father served in Vietnam. A fact my father has never once mentioned to me in his entire life. Still to this day I haven't brought this up to him, although otherwise he is quite proud of his naval service, and I know that he was on the aircraft carrier that picked up Apollo 11, or maybe it was Apollo 10, the one that came before, the dress rehearsal for the moon landing.

I still flash back to that period when my uncle was dying, when he would sit on that rocking chair in the living room and talk to us. How proud he was of the tomatoes he grew in his garden out back, and how he would place the small new tomatoes on the windowsill to ripen. And when he was dying and undergoing chemotherapy, which happened at the same time, he had almost no appetite, except he still loved to eat his sliced tomatoes. He could still really taste them, he said. Just the other day I watched my daughter Leo enjoy a tomato for the first time, stabbing at it carefully with her fork and missing, then aiming once again, picking the piece of tomato from the fork and popping it into her mouth, and I flashed back to my uncle's illness. Perhaps it's strange or morbid to acknowledge enjoying the moments bound to when our loved ones are dying, but there can be a slowness and tenderness there, a form of attention and openness that is so different from the hurried way we usually treat one another. I wonder why among my siblings I am the one to hold the hand of our elders as they lay dying, and wonder how many more deaths I will have to witness in my lifetime.

It was during this period of time when I took the trip to Springfield, Illinois, before my uncle's sudden illness and death, that I began formally composing the book on my mother, by transcribing my journals, and by beginning an interrogation over email and over the phone with my father and his sister, the remaining historians of the family. I wanted information about my great-aunt and great-grandmother, who both spent time in Illinois asylums, including at the notorious state hospitals in Elgin and Manteno. There is another version of the book, that I often think I should have written, where I would have explored in person these haunted emptied sites, which might have brought forth other memories. Like driving to my cousin Rosie's and her partner Pam's wakes in Elgin, Illinois, and feeling that Elgin, Illinois might be the worst place on earth in which to die. Or driving with my family when I was a child for hours up to Manteno to visit my grandmother's brother, who would die there, at the main campus that was eventually turned into a veteran's hospital, the same site where my great-grandmother most likely convalesced in one of the now-shuttered cottages. There are websites, devoted to the ghosts of Manteno State Hospital, photographs of these emptied spooked-out structures, where I have spent many hours getting lost. Perhaps this is why I began to read books about Mary Todd Lincoln's bizarre and convoluted insanity trial, which I began to conflate with how my great-grandmother was committed by her son in the 1930s, after a period of what was seen as extreme grief following her husband's death. A trial was held on May 19, 1875 because of an 1867 bill passed into Illinois law that guaranteed that all people accused of insanity, even wives, had the right to a public hearing. A knock on her door. I have got some bad news for you, Mrs. Lincoln, your friends have with great unanimity come to the conclusion that the troubles you have been called to pass through have been too much and produced mental disease. The president's widow was forcibly taken to the courthouse. Her lawyer, selected by her son Robert, did not contest the case. Seventeen witnesses testified to Mary Todd Lincoln's behavior. Five were doctors. The first witness called to Mary Todd Lincoln's trial was her gynecologist, who said she suffered from nervous derangement. He testified that she had a delusion about her coffee being poisoned.

She was also possessed, the doctor said, with the idea that some spirit was working in her head and taking wires out of her eyes, particularly the left one. A maid at the Grand Pacific Hotel, where Mrs. Lincoln was staying, testified that Mrs. Lincoln complained of hearing voices through the wall. Allegedly she paid maids to stay in her room because she did not want to be alone. Once, half-dressed, she entered an elevator thinking it was a washroom. She told the manager the South Side was on fire. She sent her luggage to Milwaukee to avoid it being burned. Robert, her son, testified that Mother has been of unsound mind since the death of Father. He was the star witness, a future secretary of war under Garfield. On the stand he recounted both his father's assassination and the death of his eighteen-year-old-brother Tad. Mary did not testify and no witness spoke on her behalf. The final verdict: We, the Undersigned Jurors, are satisfied that Mary Todd Lincoln is insane.

I wonder whether I wrote *Book of Mutter* partially to attempt to figure out my father's obsession with American history as well, especially military and presidential history. Although he didn't want to talk about our family's ghosts, especially the recent institutionalizing of my mother as she was dying of cancer, in those early years of writing the book my father was happy to speak with me about Mary Todd Lincoln. He has probably read every biography there is of Abraham Lincoln. When my father was not around and I was in the family house, sleuthing through old photo albums, taking an inventory of my mother's porcelain figurines, I also would go through the few books in the house, which were mostly my father's *The Civil War: An Illustrated History* from TIME magazine, as my family did not own many books, but borrowed most of their reading materials from the library. I became enraged at the time—as that was the feeling the project began with—with the official American history books, absent of death and slavery and madness, just like I felt my father and my family—whoever makes these records—were attempting to erase my mother's life, and what had happened to her at the end of her life. The sense of injustice that energized my writing when I began was connected to a deep sense of injustice about how women have been treated throughout history. What other disobedient women in history were sane at one point, until driven mad through despair and rage? Or whose despair and rage was branded irrational? This originally led me into a period of research into architectures of insanity, from Foucault's history of madness and his chronology of La Salpêtrière, including how Philippe Pinel treated the largely indigent female population of the public hospital according to 19th century concepts of moral insanity, leading to Charcot's clinical style, documenting the theatrical stages of the female hysteric later on in the century. This led into research into the local history of the Illinois asylum, which had internalized the French concept of *traitement moral.* I read a book called *Illinois Public Mental Health Services: 1847–2000* while sitting at one of the wooden tables in the reading room at the Newberry Library, copying down notes and captions under photographs such as "basket making structured patients' time." Most of this was removed from the book, ultimately, only surviving in traces. I also researched the Illinois Asylum for Feeble-minded Children, in Lincoln, Illinois, where a young Henry Darger was confined and ultimately escaped, claiming he walked back to Chicago the 100 miles on foot, writing later in his 500-page memoirs that it was during this journey that he witnessed the tornado named Sweetie Pie that would shape his personal mythology, as I write in the book on my mother. I imagine another book on my mother—a book of serious nonfiction that could be nominated for awards—where I take a walking tour of various sites in Illinois, just like Sebald does in *Rings of Saturn* in the Suffolk countryside, tracing after various histories of madness and destruction through architecture and its absences. Perhaps that is the reason for these stutters of American history and Lincoln memorabilia in the book that remains—I am searching after Illinois history, as Susan Howe writes, to "trust the place to inform the voice." But as I continued working on the book, I didn't live in Illinois any longer, and had no desire to return, and little reason, as most everyone was dead, or had moved, and my father came regularly to New York to visit.

When reading about Mary Todd Lincoln, I was drawn to what was seen as her extravagant reactions to grief, like when her 11-year-old son Willie died from typhoid fever while they were living in the White House. At the time her husband warned her that if she didn't snap out of it he would have her committed. She began to shop excessively as a way to ward off loss. Shopping sprees and goods on credit during austerity campaigns. A bill for over $600 for the purchase of eighty-four pairs of gloves. She was in over $70,000 of debt, which she hid from her spouse, a debt that she petitioned Congress to purchase for her when her husband was assassinated. She wrote, "I am passing through a very painful ordeal which the country, in remembrances of my noble and devoted husband, should have spared me." This extravagance was seen as a sign of her declining mental health during her trial. Sales clerks testified to her purchases. She bought three watches for Robert, several sets of lace curtains, and sets of gloves and handkerchiefs. But her attempts to barter on the price for the gloves and the handkerchiefs were seen as another sign of impending madness. Also when the widow attempted to pawn her jewelry and wardrobe to try to pay off massive debts. Once the newspapers discovered that Mrs. Lincoln was attempting to sell her furs, laces, jewelry and dresses in New York under the pseudonym of "Mrs. Clark" and through the brokerage of one "Mr. Brady," they had a field day. The spectacle of the unraveling woman.

Invoice of articles sent to Mrs. A. Lincoln:

> 1 Trunk
> 1 Lace Dress
> 1 do.do flounced
> 5 Lace Shawls
> 3 Camel hair shawls
> 1 Lace parasol cover
> 1 do. Handkerchief
> 1 Sable boa.
> 1 White do.
> 1 Set furs.
> 2 Paisley Shawls
> 2 Gold bracelets
> 16 dresses
> 2 Opera cloaks
> 1 Purple Shawl
> 1 Feather cape
> 28 yds silk
>
> ARTICLES SOLD
> 1 Diamond ring.
> 3 Small do.
> 1 Set furs.

1 Camel hair shawl.
1 Red do.
2 Dresses.
1 Child's Shawl.
1 Lace Shantilly Shawl

I was drawn to the verticality of such a list, like the closet of my mother's clothes. A closet a kind of haunted archive. In previous versions of the book, I had long lists of clothes, such as an auction of Marilyn Monroe's belongings, a public breakdown broken into saleable pieces. When a woman can be made into a museum. When writing about this shameful event in Mary Todd Lincoln's widowed life, dubbed "The Old Clothes Scandal" by the press, in drafts of the book that were then deleted from the final book on my mother, I drew heavily on the memoir of her confidante and modiste, Elizabeth Keckley. In the memoir, *Behind the Scenes: Or Thirty Years a Slave, and Four Years in the White House*, Keckley begins recounting being born into slavery, charged at the age of four years old with taking care of a baby, and being lashed when she accidentally dropped the infant. In the short opening pages she tells almost matter-of-factly of vicious whippings, being raped by her master, bearing his child. Then rising in rank from dressing the society women of St. Louis to her time in the White House. These early reflections quickly moved from her early autobiography to her interactions with this First Lady, how she dressed her, how she agreed to assist in the wardrobe sale once the former first lady was destitute and in debt (Mrs. Lincoln, in letters, begging, MY DEAR LIZZIE, *please help*). A lifetime of self-reliance compared to her employer's personal chaos. Every event was filtered through

Keckley's memory of what her employer wore, in her exacting, lush description of the clothes. "For the inauguration, Mrs. Lincoln looked elegant in her rose-colored moiré-antique. She wore a pearl necklace, pearl ear-rings, pearl bracelets, and red roses in her hair." A New York newspaper about the auction notes that although the black silk dress worn by Mary Todd Lincoln on the night of the assassination was presented, the other articles that adorned her on that night are now the property of Keckley, the earrings, the bonnet, and the black velvet cloak still blood-splattered and now dried and never able to be removed, notes the reporter, and kept as a *memento mori*. "When her son Willie was dying, I arranged Mrs. Lincoln's hair, and then assisted her to dress. Her dress was white satin, trimmed with black lace." The New York newspapers noted in detail the wear and stains of the clothes on auction. "MY DEAR KECKLEY," Mary Todd Lincoln writes in a telegram, with her characteristic tone. "I sometimes wish myself out of this world of sorrow and care. I fear my fine articles at B.'s are getting pulled to pieces and soiled." I am now thinking to the end of Sebald's *Rings of Saturn*, when after a long passage about the Nazi sericulture industry—charting the transformation of the silkworm through the entire book—he notes the Victorian practice of laying black mourning silk over landscapes. How *Rings of Saturn* reads in such a way, a black mourning silk over a landscape, or like the stiff garment worn by Dürer's angel of melancholy, which Sebald conjures up in the first part, thinking about a friend who has recently died, a Flaubert scholar, who would sit bent over her chair in her office, surrounded by papers, scribbling notes. I attempted to weave through these moments, the black silks of mourning, of American history in the book on my mother, and I failed.

When Elizabeth Keckley published her memoir, Robert Lincoln bought up as many published copies as he could find and had them destroyed. I was compelled, at the time, how past the initial pages, Keckley's gaze was not on her past, but rather on the life of her famous employer, and that Keckley's life only came through in flashes. That moment of coming to terms with a possible betrayal at the beginning of her book, in writing a book on another: "If these ladies could say everything about the wife of the President, why should I not be permitted to lay her secret history bare?" I'm beginning to wonder if there is always some level of betrayal in writing the stories of another. It felt wrong to use Elizabeth Keckley's memoir as a way to get to Mary Todd Lincoln, and this is why ultimately I removed these sections from the final manuscript. I have been having an ongoing conversation with my friend Sofia about how Sebald in *Rings of Saturn* subverts somehow the ventriloquism of historical fiction, in that his narrator is always an "I," always encountering these historical figures through their documentation and archives, although the ways that Sebald uses first-person is a sort of ventriloquism as an intended and ghostly effect, such as in the section of Roger Casement and Joseph Conrad in the Congo. Quite often in *Rings of Saturn* and elsewhere Sebald channels monologues of historical figures that he sees as doubles, as in the case of Conrad. As Sofia theorizes to me, Sebald never tries to step into the mind of a Congolese labourer, which could possibly feel appropriative (although, she notes later, since Sebald's mode of characterization is by channeling documents, since the documents of a Congolese labourer from that period wouldn't exist, that would be impossible anyway). Although, I wrote Sofia today, having recently reread *Rings of Saturn*, isn't Sebald still reifying a colonialist gaze, allied with the figure of the white savior? But then, Sofia returns, is there a good or pure way for Sebald, in his position, to have written about the Congo anyway? Perhaps this is something we have to accept as colonial legacy, this is why writing about history, Sofia writes me, is so hard. It's horrible, this responsibility for the stories of others. When I originally began this dialogue with Sofia two years ago about the Elizabeth Keckley and Mary Todd sections of the book on my mother, whether it's wrong to include them and wrong to remove them, she suggested perhaps that these sections could be a powerful way for me to write my experience as a white woman in this country, as Sebald writes of his belonging to Germany through stories of colonialism and Jewish death. But then the question becomes, she writes, is that your goal? To write your experience as a white woman? The truth was I didn't admire, or identify with Mary Todd Lincoln, and even though I admired Elizabeth Keckley, I wasn't sure how to explore either of their narratives in the book on my mother. Was I attempting a philosophy of history, like Sebald was in *Rings of Saturn*? I believe there were ghost iterations of the book on my mother in which I was, and perhaps these attempts towards witness, still remain, in the book on my mother. Maybe what's needed is to write with the awareness of being wrong. Can one's own wrongness be a source of compassion? Sofia writes to me today. And yet I can see a possible book, the book I should have written, that was not about my mother or about my father, but about the stutters of American history, where I wrestled with my uncertainties, where I came to terms with my wrongness, where I thought tenderly through the lives of others, not in ways that served my own project, but where I served them, and thought through them, where I was the ghost, hovering over, attempting....attempting what? Perhaps just attempting to come closer.

Appendix K

MUSEUM OF THE HISTORY OF HUMAN SUFFERING

The original reason I began this project was to speak about what was absent or abandoned from the final published version of *Book of Mutter*, yet I have only circled around this. There is a cursory list of these errors and omissions in the back of the published book. I was surprised, when people have read the book, that this is often what they have wanted to talk about.

When I go back and look at this list in a PDF of what I think is the final layout, I realize that there are several words misspelled. I'm not sure whether they were caught at some point. When I wrote the materials for the back of the book, I was heavily pregnant and still commuting upstate for several hours each way to teach. Plus there was an Italian man living upstairs who drummed all day long, and I couldn't think well with all of the drumming, certainly not to proof-read. I wrote this list off the top of my head. I realize now scanning this list that I've only touched on a few elements in this entire book, this book that was not supposed to be a book that has become a book.

I realize the major thread, or threads, that were taken out of the published version of *Book of Mutter* mostly deal with atrocity and history. The ethics of paying witness, of writing about another's pain. This is what remains to think through, and yet I am resistant. Still I want to ask myself this question, like I am on trial. Why was I so drawn to documenting suffering in this book about my mother? And why did I remove it?

* * *

I have been watching the beginning of *Hiroshima mon amour* over and over again on my laptop, taking notes. The two shots at the opening, the dying bodies, covered with ash, dissolving to the two lovers, their smooth, sweaty, naked flesh. The ash turns to sweat like glitter. What is the effect of this texture, of this layering and dissolve? The dialogue that follows also crosses boundaries, the woman's extreme identification with the victims of Hiroshima. I read somewhere that Marguerite Duras based this woman on the phenomenon of white Western women with broken hearts who flocked to the Hiroshima Peace Memorial Museum in the years after the war. The actress, played by Emmanuelle Riva, is an actress there in Hiroshima to shoot a peace film. We learn, later, that her lover was a German soldier shot dead, and she went mad, she was shamed in the middle of the town square, her head shaved, and she was kept in the family cellar until the end of the war. In a dreamy, lover's voice, the man, a Japanese architect played by Eiji Okada, who has lost his entire family to the atomic bomb, says: "You saw nothing in Hiroshima. Nothing." The white French woman says: "I saw everything." Then we're in her point of view, with exteriors. "I saw the hospital—I'm sure of it. The hospital in Hiroshima exists. How could I not have seen it?" The reenactment of sick women in kimonos in bed, a naked back of a man turns, covered in scars. The man's voice: "You didn't see the hospital in Hiroshima. You saw nothing in Hiroshima." She: "Four times at the museum." Exterior shot of museum. "I saw people walking around. People walk around, lost in thought, among the photographs. The reconstructions, for lack of anything else." She repeats: "The photographs, the photographs. The reconstructions, for lack of anything else. The explanations, for lack of anything else." She keeps repeating: Four times at the museum at Hiroshima. The exhibits of a museum: the twisted metal. The bouquet of bottle caps. The twisted bicycle. Objects of horror aestheticized like modern sculptures. "Anonymous masses of hair, that the women of Hiroshima, upon waking in the morning, would find had fallen out."

"I was hot in Peace Square. 10,000 degrees in Peace Square." The woman says to the man, who has lost his entire family because of the bomb. I haven't yet watched this part of the film this time, but I know the woman will repeat, "I. Am. Hiroshima." Which recalls the line removed from Sylvia Plath's "Lady Lazarus," that I have heard read in her stern glamorous dictation in a BBC Radio recording: "I may be skin and bones. I may be Japanese."

I think it was the chapter on *Hiroshima mon amour* in Cathy Caruth's book on trauma, that made me incorporate it into early drafts of *Book of Mutter*. Caruth thinking through the relationship between history and the body. "What do the dying bodies of the past—the dying bodies of Hiroshima—have to do with the living bodies of the present?" I was interested in how personal experiences of trauma could be conflated with collective suffering. I was interested particularly in the ethics of that conflation, in colliding an individual consciousness with experiences of war and atrocity.

Rewatching *Hiroshima mon amour*, it doesn't feel like a work about witness. It instead privileges the white Western woman's wartime experiences of trauma and madness. Hiroshima feels like a historical setting to enact her own woundedness. The woman, speaking Duras's words, doesn't seem to be feeling true empathy for the victims of atrocity even as she says, I have felt what they have felt, I have experienced this pain. Even as she says, See my smooth flesh—it is scarred on the inside.

* * *

Bhanu Kapil's *Ban en Banlieue* differently reenacts a series of memorials to martyrs of violence, of racism and patriarchy, through the layering of identification and how the body can reenact and perform history. At the end of the work, encounter becomes ventriloquism—not only the instability of whether the narrator is or is not "Ban," the brown/black girl walking home in a London suburb on the day of the race riots, but also as Kapil traces the narrator "I" who becomes the story of the widow who commits *sati* (the ritual act of a widow immolating herself on her husband's funeral pyre). Perhaps this is because *Ban en Banlieue* also asks the questions: How can a memorial have the energy of performance? How can writing pay witness in the present, thinking through bodies within history?

In *The Art of Cruelty*, Maggie Nelson, thinking through this distance and immersion in the work of Sylvia Plath and Kara Walker, quotes Adrian Piper delineating these distinctions: "Vicarious possession (case where we take one's perspective to be our own) vs self-absorption (where we project our own pre-occupations onto another)."

* * *

I would visit Doris Salcedo's 1996 installation *Atrabiliarios* at the Akron Art Museum, when I lived in that city, and was working on the book. A ritual space become reliquary. Rectangular holes covered by translucent cow bladder vellum sewn to the wall, the stitches like a body sewn back together after an autopsy. Each niche contains one or two shoes. Shoes sometimes the only means to identify bodies found in a mass grave (the pain of seeing these, a *punctum*). In her essay, "Against Witness," Cathy Park Hong writes about Salcedo's installations, which utilize ritualistic objects, especially garments and furniture to recall the disappeared in Salcedo's home of Bogotá, Colombia, but also other dead around the world, a constant dislocated grief. She writes that Salcedo's installations act as a "second witness" and are not appropriative because they do not show bodies. When writing this, Hong is thinking through Sontag's second book of photography, *Regarding the Pain of Others*, her thesis on the erotic appetite of showing pictures of bodies in pain. The passage in which Sontag writes about the famous photograph of Fou-Tchou-Li, as he suffers from *lingchi*, or death by a thousand cuts. Sontag lingers on this photograph, on Georges Bataille writing of meditating on the ecstasy of this image, the slowness of this extreme suffering. She attempts to understand the contemplation of this image. Not the man, not his pain, but the image, and Bataille's understanding of it.

How wary Sontag is of photographs of war. In her tract she writes of how these iconic images of war can fix memory, can actually work against thinking. She critically references Sebald's use of a photograph of the mass grave in Bergen-Belsen in *Rings of Saturn*. A photo originally without context, like Francis Bacon's photocollage of atrocities that he paints from that Maggie Nelson takes issue with in *The Art of Cruelty*. The Bergen-Belsen image in the Sebald obscenely echoing the photographs of other bodily forms in the book (like the masses of silkworms). For photographs of deformed bodies can be beautiful too, Sontag writes. Is that their danger, their aesthetic resonance?

During the early years when I was working on the manuscript, I was reading Elaine Scarry's *The Body in Pain*, an intellectual leftover from my graduate work thinking about performance art and pain (Marina Abramovic's *Rhythm 0*, Ana Mendieta's *Rape Piece*, the suspension hangings of Stelarc). I was struck by not only her thinking on the failure of torture methods to provide true confessions, as well as what she writes of the impossibility of empathy, of truly grasping the interiority of a body in pain. How when the body is in pain, subjectivity leaves. One becomes object: "the body."

I forgot that when first writing the book, over many years, I was conflating my mother and the Iraq war. Personal and collective history dissolved. How her wake was held during the bombing of Baghdad. Is this why I was so obsessed with the photographs of Abu Ghraib, with why Lynndie England took those photographs? With Alberto Gonzalez's lying, his willed forgetting (the repeated erasure: "I do not recall.")? With the memos of the Bush administration. With the testimony of The Tipton Three and The Quahtani Logs in The Torture Archive. With the shattering of language in torture, with the dismissal or erasure of the suffering body in official records. Jenny Holzer's Redaction Paintings series, that I saw at the Museum of Contemporary Art in Chicago. How redaction is the opposite of witness. How I wanted to write of how others suffer, how others are erased, how others are forgotten. But my mother too. My mother perhaps most of all. I cut out all of these notes and now I have these other notes. These fragments. And still I will have to go over all of this again, in more depth, at some other time.

— KZ, April 21, 2018

Acknowledgments

I would like to acknowledge everyone that invited me to give these talks—Printed Matter (Stephanie LaCava especially), Duke University (Aarthi Vadde and Kelly Wooten especially), The Renaissance Society (especially Karsten Lund), Washington University as part of the "The Critic as Artist/The Artist as Critic" Hurst initiative (especially Danielle Dutton, Melanie Micir, and Martin Riker), The Poetry Project (especially Mirene Arsanios), and CalArts School of Critical Studies. Thanks to Hannah Gold at *Berlin Quarterly* for publishing Appendix B, Francesca Wade at *The White Review* for publishing Appendix F, and Hunter Braithwaite at *Affidavit* for publishing Appendix G. Profound gratitude to Hedi El Kholti and Chris Kraus for giving this itinerant work as well as *Book of Mutter* and *Heroines* a home at Semiotext(e). To everyone at MIT Press. To Mel Flashman, for her patience. To Emma Kirby and Sorcha Gannon, who watched Leo as I wrote several of these talks in those early months, and for their conversation. To Julie Moon, for her conversation and careful read and for helping to watch Leo as I attempted to edit this book. Love to Sofia Samatar, whose friendship and writing has catalyzed my thinking the past two years, and whose conversation made this project come into existence. To Suzanne Scanlon, Danielle Dutton, Amina Cain, Stephanie LaCava, and Adrian Nathan West, for helping me to think through things, and for their friendship. To Alexander Pines, for his conversation and for driving to Chicago just to attend one of these talks. To Bhanu Kapil, for allowing me to commune with her not only as a friend but also as a reader. To Moyra Davey, for her writing and work that's been so important to me the past two years. To T Clutch Fleischmann, for the example of their own thinking and writing, for their read of this book, and their friendship. Admiration and gratitude to Kate Briggs, for her writing and translations, and for her advance remarks on this project. To B. Ingrid Olson for the art she created especially for the cover, and for the conversation and collaboration over the past year. And of course I want to acknowledge my partner, the writer and artist John Vincler, who gave up his job to be at home so that I could continue writing, who has often sacrificed working on his own writing so I could work on mine, who is my first reader, editor, and the main person that I think with.

Kate Zambreno is the author of the novels *Green Girl* and *O Fallen Angel* as well as the nonfiction *Heroines* and *Book of Mutter* (both published by Semiotexte(e)).